Growing up with Grammar 4

First published in Australia in 2003 by New Frontier Publishing
Revised and reprinted in 2005, 2008
ABN 67 126 171 757
Unit 4 Building 7 49 Frenchs Forest Rd, Frenchs Forest NSW 2086 Australia
www.newfrontier.com.au

Cover Illustrations: Marion Kim,   Internal Illustrations: Jason Knight

Designed by Ronald Proft

Edited by Kristina Proft

National Library of Australia
Cataloguing-in-Publication data:
Winch, Gordon, 1930-.
Growing Up with Grammar. Book 4

1. English language – Grammar – Juvenile literature.
2. English language – Usage – Juvenile literature.
3. English language – Writing – Juvenile literature.

428

13 Digit ISBN 9780975089699

Acknowledgments
The author would like to thank Lesley Ljungdahl and Paul March,
who acted as academic consultants to this series.

The author would also like to thank the principals and staff of the schools
throughout Australia who assisted in the research leading to the publication of
the *Growing up with Grammar* series and the *Primary Grammar Dictionary*.

Special thanks are offered to the following schools:
Beecroft Public School, North Rocks Public School, Northmead Public School,
Pymble Ladies' College, Ravenswood School for Girls, St Gerard's Primary School,
Sydney Grammar Preparatory School and The Hills Grammar School.

Text Acknowledgments
Grahame, Kenneth, *The Wind in the Willows*, Methuen, London, 1908.
Pausacker, Jenny, *The Go-Cart Kids*, Reading Rigby, Adelaide, 1981.

Printed in China through by Hung Hing Offset Printing

Growing up with Grammar 4

Gordon Winch

Contents

To the Student

Growing up with Grammar is an interesting book for you to use. I think you will enjoy working through it. There are many different things to read and many activities to do.

What's more, you will learn about grammar, which will help you in all kinds of ways at school.

Grammar has not always been popular with students but I am hoping that this book will make it "top of the pops". In particular, I want you to be more like the second student in the following poem, not like the kids in the first verse!

Grammar

Some kids think grammar's really YUK!
It's boring and it's tough;
And learning it's like climbing cliffs;
The going's very rough.

But I think grammar's heaps of fun,
(I never have enough),
And learning it is just a breeze;
It's SCINTILLATING stuff!

Have fun!

Gordon Winch

To the Teacher

What the book is

Growing up with Grammar, Book 4 is the fourth book of four in the *Growing up with Grammar* series that covers the requirements of the primary grammar syllabus in grammar, punctuation and usage with special focus on outcomes and indicators. Book 4 is set at the level of Stage 3 of the NSW Syllabus, English K–6.

Why it was written

The series has been written and published following serious research into need and demand in Australian primary schools.

The author

The author is Dr Gordon Winch, a well-known writer and authority in the field of educational texts in English.

What the book contains

Book 4 contains 32 units that teach concepts of grammar, punctuation and usage in the context of a section of text, across a range of Key Learning Areas. Each unit covers a double-page spread and provides clear definitions of grammatical points followed by interesting and varied exercises. "More Action" segments provide follow-on work at the end of each unit. A reference section on Text Types, in the form of an appendix, provides an interchange between theory and practice. This section is designed to help students with both their writing and grammar. Cross-references to the Text Type section are made in each of the units.

How the grammar is sequenced

The grammar is taught in Levels, following the sequence Word Level; Phrase and Group Level; Clause and Sentence Level; and Text Level. Correct Word Usage, Figurative Language amd Punctuation follow the grammar segments.

Assessment and monitoring

Revision and testing pages are provided at various places in the book to assess the learned material, and outcomes and indicators checklists are also provided at the end of the book. An answer section facilitates individual use of the text and is a resource for the teacher.

**How to use
the book**

The book can be used in a variety of ways: as a text book for each student at a particular level, as a resource for teachers and students who are following a loose-leaf portfolio approach, and as a valuable homework grammar text. Its simple structure will allow the teacher to fit the book into his or her program with ease.

It is important to note that the text and others in the series can be used in a number of grades depending on the learning requirements of different schools, classes and students. It is specially designed for flexible use.

For instance, two different books in the series may be used in some classrooms or one particular book may be used over two years. The material is carefully graded, developmental and covers the primary school syllabus fully.

**Primary
Grammar
Dictionary**

The *Growing up with Grammar* series is complementary to the *Primary Grammar Dictionary*. This Dictionary provides easy and immediate reference to all the grammar, punctuation and usage in the *Growing Up with Grammar* series, plus definitions of many other terms and concepts that are found in traditional and functional grammars. It is an essential resource for every student and every teacher. The Dictionary covers the grammar, punctuation and correct word usage requirements of the primary school, from kindergarten/prep. to Year 6.

Overview
The Book at a Glance

32 double-page units of grammar, punctuation and usage

- Covering syllabus content outcomes and indicators at Stage 3
- In context of literary and factual text types over Key Learning Areas
- At word, phrase and group, clause and sentence and text levels
- With grammar definitions, text excerpts, varied exercises and "More Action" activities.

4 double-page revision units with "Take A Test" focus

Answer section to all questions

Outcomes and indicators checklists for assessment

Text type description appendix with cross-reference.

Outcomes	Talking and Listening	TS3.1, TS3.2, TS3.3, TS3.4	(See p. 89)
	Reading	RS3.5, RS3.6 RS3.7, RS3.8	
	Writing	WS3.9, WS3.10, WS3.13, WS3.14	

Indicators (See p. 90)

Key Learning Areas
- Creative Arts K–6
- English K–6
- Human Society and Its Environment K–6
- Personal Development Health and Physical Education K–6
- Science and Technology K–6

Text Type:

FACTUAL RECOUNT

NOUNS: COMMON, PROPER, COLLECTIVE

A **noun** is the name of a person, place or thing, like *whales*, *Sunday* or *sheep*. **Common nouns** are the names of common things like *gulls*. They start with small letters. **Proper nouns** are the names of special people, places or things, like *Joanna* or *Sunday*, and start with capital letters. **Collective nouns** are the names of groups or collections of things, like *pod* or *flock* in the phrase a *pod of whales* or a *flock of gulls*.

A Pod of Whales

Last Sunday, Joanne, Danny Correto and I went to White Horse Beach and saw a pod of whales frolicking near the shore. A flock of gulls was circling overhead and a school of fish kept jumping out of the sea.

We went out to see the whales in a tiny convoy of boats, but we were not allowed to come too close to the whales. They might have thought that we were like a silly flock of sheep – all peering at them as they played in the sea.

1. Write nouns from the factual recount to fill the places in the table. Write each noun only once. (See Factual Recount, p. 87.)

COMMON	PROPER	COLLECTIVE

2. Find as many small common nouns as you can in the compound nouns in the box. Write them down. The first two are done for you. Write each small noun once only.

seahorse	catfish	whalebone	starfish	seaweed
fishpond	headland	sandbag	shoreline	boathouse

sea, horse _____

_____

_____

3. Match each collective noun to a common noun. The first one is done for you.

crowd	elephants
bunch	pearls
swarm	actors
string	horses
stable	planes
troupe	scones
herd	athletes
batch	bees
squadron	people
team	grapes

4. Finish these sentences with nouns from the box.

gaggle   **swarm**   **groups**   **Captain Bagshaw**   **herd**

_____ was in charge of the boats. He insisted that

_____ of people should sit quietly and not behave like a _____

of geese, a _____ of cattle or a _____ of insects.

5. Provide a proper noun for each of these categories. The first one is done for you.

country _____Spain_____ ; river _____ ; mountain _____ ;

town _____ ; capital _____ ; famous artist _____ ;

favourite movie _____ ; favourite singer _____ .

MORE ACTION

- Make a list of common nouns that are things you would (a) take to the beach, (b) wear to a party, (c) take to school, or (d) take on holidays.
- Make up some amusing collective nouns of your own like *a purr of kittens, a yap of dogs, a wriggle of worms* or *a croak of frogs*. Share your collective nouns with others in your class. Have a competition to see which ones are the best.

Text Type:

EXPOSITION

ABSTRACT NOUNS

Abstract nouns, like all nouns, are the names of things, but abstract nouns exist only in the mind. You cannot actually touch, taste, hear, smell or see them. Examples are *happiness, loneliness, joy* and *sadness*.

Happiness is a State of Mind

Some people can experience happiness while others would be in despair. A hermit, for instance, may find joy in living alone while others would suffer misery.

Again, some people find excitement in dangerous situations while others feel only fear and distress.

It certainly depends on the person. Happiness, like many other of our feelings, is a state of mind.

1. Read through the above exposition and underline all the abstract nouns you can find. (See Exposition, p. 86.) *Happiness* is the first one.

2. Write the abstract noun that is as near as possible to the opposite of the words in the list. Pick the answers from the box. The first one is done for you.

cruelty	hopelessness	unhappiness
boredom	hate	ugliness

a. happiness   _____unhappiness_____

b. hope   _____

c. kindness   _____

d. beauty   _____

e. love   _____

f. excitement   _____

3. Write five abstract nouns to match each of the faces. Pick from the box.

joy   exhilaration   excitement   grief   despair
happiness   misery   exuberance   hopelessness   sadness

a.   b.

_____   _____

_____   _____

_____   _____

_____   _____

_____   _____

4. Put these abstract nouns in pairs. The first pair is done for you.

joy   doubt   sadness   happiness   misery   hate
bravery   love   uncertainty   loathing   affection   courage

joy happiness		

5. Make abstract nouns from these adjectives. The first one is done for you.

painful _____ pain _____   sad _____

lonely _____   healthy _____

pitiful _____   sorrowful _____

beautiful _____   angry _____

courageous _____   greedy _____

MORE ACTION

• In your own book or folder, write five sentences that contain the following abstract nouns: *joy, despair, greed, affection, anger.*

UNIT 3

NOUNS: NUMBER AND GENDER

Nouns have **number**. They can be singular or plural. Singular means one; plural means more than one. *Mammal* is singular; *mammals* is plural. Nouns also have **gender**. They may be masculine gender (male) as in *bull*, or feminine gender (female), as in *cow*. If a noun is neither masculine nor feminine gender, it is said to be neuter gender, as in *milk* or *earth*. Some nouns, like *platypus* or *echidna* can be masculine, feminine or both. We say these nouns have a common gender. For **case**, see **Pronouns: Case** (Unit 11).

Australian Mammals

Mammals are animals whose babies feed on milk from the mother. For example, cows and bulls are mammals. The cow feeds her calf on her milk.

There are many Australian mammals that are unique on earth. The platypus, the echidna, the wombat and the kangaroo are all mammals with special qualities. Just think of the female platypus. She lays eggs like reptiles do, but she is a mammal, nevertheless. She feeds her babies with milk from her body . . .

1. Circle all the plural nouns in the above information report. (See Information Report, p. 87.) Underline all the singular nouns.

2. Write **M** for masculine, **F** for feminine, **N** for neuter and **C** for common beside these words from the information report, *Australian Mammals*.

mother _____   animals   _____

milk _____   kangaroo_____

cows_____   bulls   _____

mammals _____   babies _____

platypus _____   earth   _____

3. Finish these sentences with plural nouns. For example, *lady, ladies*.

a. The_____(baby) drink milk from the_____(mother).

b. _____(Kangaroo) are Australian_____(mammal).

c. They have special _____(quality).

d. _____(Sheep) and_____(horse) are not native to Australia.

4. What do mammals eat? Here are some tricky words that cause trouble when we form the plural. Write the plural of each one.

SINGULAR	PLURAL	SINGULAR	PLURAL
tomato	_____	leaf	_____
berry	_____	larva	_____
potato	_____	fish	_____
grass	_____	mango	_____

5. Write the plural form of these creatures.

sheep	_____	mouse	_____
goose	_____	butterfly	_____
echidna	_____	turkey	_____
wolf	_____	monkey	_____
ox	_____	fly	_____

6. Write the feminine form of these creatures.

stallion	_____	ram	_____
drake	_____	gander	_____
rooster	_____	bull	_____
boar	_____	rabbit	_____
lion	_____	dog	_____

MORE ACTION

- Write the plural names of as many Australian mammals as you know.
- Look in your dictionary to find the exact meaning of *mammal, marsupial, crustacean, invertebrate* and *reptile*. Write a short information report about one of them.
- Remember these tricky plurals: for hoof it is hoofs or hooves; for roof, only roofs.

UNIT 4

ADJECTIVES: DESCRIPTIVE, NUMERAL, POSSESSIVE

Adjectives are describing words. They describe (add meaning) to a noun or pronoun, as in *sharp* knife or *chilly* winter. **Descriptive adjectives** tell us about the qualities of a person or thing, as in *sharp* light or *chilly* morning. Two other types of adjectives are **numeral (numbering) adjectives**, as in *two* horsemen, and **possessive adjectives**, that show ownership, as in *their* heavy saddles. Possessive adjectives are also called pronominal adjectives because they are part pronoun.

The Two Horsemen

The first sharp rays of chilly daylight silhouetted the dark forms of the two horsemen who were making their steady way up the rocky slope of the bare and inhospitable mountain. Their riding gear hid their particular identity, age and gender: broad-brimmed hats, oilskin coats and spurred boots seemed identical. The lonely riders were cloned intruders on a desolate landscape that wintry day. Their steaming horses . . .

1. Read through this literary description. (See Literary Description, p. 82.)

   a. Underline all the descriptive adjectives you can find. The first two are *sharp* and *chilly*.

   b. Circle the numeral adjectives, including the repetitions.

   c. Draw boxes around the possessive adjectives, including the repetitions.

2. Add two descriptive adjectives to these nouns. Make them descriptive of the literary description, *The Two Horsemen*.

   a. _____   _____ horsemen

   b. _____   _____ light

   c. _____   _____ mountain

   d. _____   _____ hats

   e. _____   _____ coats

   f. _____   _____ boots

3. Write descriptive adjectives that would be opposites of the following. The first one is done for you.

a. cold, wintry day;_____hot,_____ _____summery_____ day

b. tiny, black horse;_____ _____ horse

c. fat, lazy dog; _____ _____ dog

d. full, heavy pack;_____ _____ pack

e. careless, thoughtless action; _____ _____ action

4. a. Finish this verse with numeral adjectives.

I have _____ eyes and _____ small nose,

_____ nails but just _____ toes.

b. Finish these sentences with possessive adjectives. Pick from the box.

my   his   her   its   our   their   your

(i) That is _____ pen. I bought it for myself. This is _____ pen. You can keep it.

(ii) They took _____ books home but I left _____ books at school.

(iii) She is _____ best friend. We often go to _____ place to play.

(iv) See that insect. It has stripes on _____ back.

5. Fit descriptive adjectives to the correct nouns. Draw lines to make the joins. The first one is done for you.

fearless	elephant
beautiful	snake
crowded	bus
slithery	student
enormous	forest
exciting	adventure
clever	flower
dense	explorer

MORE ACTION

• Look at the first page of a book you are reading. How many descriptive adjectives can you find in it?

• Imagine you are selling a computer game, a skateboard or a bike. Write your own advertisement. Use descriptive adjectives that would help you to convince buyers.

• Find better words to replace *good* and *bad* in these phrases:
a good movie; a bad experience.

Text Type:

EXPLANATION

ADJECTIVES: CLASSIFYING, MODAL

A **classifying** adjective tells us the class of the noun it describes, such as *native* plants or *eucalyptus* trees.

You can pick out a classifying adjective because it will not take the word "very" in front of it: you cannot say "a very *eucalyptus* tree", whereas you could say "a very *big* tree".

Modal adjectives show amounts of probability or certainty. A *possible* action is not as certain as a *definite* action. Both of these types of adjectives are describing words.

Why Native Plants are Best

Native plants are best in our Australian environment because they have become acclimatised to it. They can cope with possible droughts and certain bushfires. Gum trees or eucalyptus trees, as they are called, are definite examples of hardy Australian flora. There would be only a slight chance that imported species would survive where our native trees do well . . .

1. In the above part of an explanation of *Why Native Plants Are Best*, there are underlined adjectives. (See Explanation, p. 85.) Write them in the correct columns. You do not have to repeat "Australian".

CLASSIFYING	MODAL

2. Pick out the classifying adjectives. Write them underneath.

pretty dress, *plastic* box, *African* elephant, *poor* person, *library* book, *tasty* pie, *sinister* behaviour, *tiger* shark, *cruel* treatment, *passenger* bus, *cotton* T-shirt, *English* lesson, *Japanese* garden, *Australian* passport, *beautiful* view, *daily* newspaper.

_____

_____

3. Use adjectives from the box to finish the sentences with high modality (probability).

> **possible   probable   definite   uncertain   sure**
> **certain   unlikely   likely   unnecessary   necessary**

a. It is _____ that we will win.

b. I am _____ about the answers.

c. A heavy storm is a very _____ happening.

d. It is _____ that I will be coming to your party.

4. Write in modal adjectives that come from these modal nouns.

MODAL NOUN	MODAL ADJECTIVE
certainty	
possibility	
probability	
necessity	
determination	

5. Finish these sentences with your own classifying or modal adjective.

Our class plants _____ shrubs and trees in the

_____ playground every year on National Tree Planting Day.

There is only a _____ chance that we would miss out.

It is raining heavily! Heavy rain in the desert is a/an _____ occurrence.

MORE ACTION

- In your own book or folder, write a paragraph which shows low probability about your chances of going to the beach on Sunday. Use words such as *uncertain, unlikely, impossible, unsure* and *doubtful*.

- Write a high probability paragraph about your belief that the school will win at the sports carnival. Use words such as *absolutely, certain, sure* and *undoubted*.

Text Type:

NARRATIVE

ADJECTIVES: DEMONSTRATIVE; DEGREE WITH ADJECTIVES

Demonstrative adjectives are pointing adjectives. They tell us what is being pointed out. The demonstrative adjectives are *this*, *that*, *these* and *those*. An example is *those* runners.

Most adjectives have **degree**. Degree shows more or less of a thing. For example, *good* is an adjective, *better* is another and *best* is another. These words show differences in degree. The three levels are called **positive**, **comparative** and **superlative** degree.

(Note that you cannot have double comparatives or superlatives, as in *more better* or *most fastest*.)

The Race

C'mon Lisa. You're the greatest. The best. You can do it.
You're faster than the others – and better trained.
You're stronger, too, even if you're small. It's a mind-set.
You're tough inside. The toughest.
Just keep thinking, those runners can't beat me. That big kid looks soft, anyway.
C'mon Lisa! You can win! Let's go!

1. a. Circle the two demonstrative adjectives in this piece from the narrative called *The Race*. (See Narrative, p. 83.)

   b. Finish this table of adjectives in the positive, comparative and superlative degrees.

POSITIVE	COMPARATIVE	SUPERLATIVE
		greatest
		best
	faster	
tough		
small		

2. Fill in the correct demonstrative adjectives.

    a. This apple is mine. _____ apple is yours.

    b. These shoes fit me. _____ shoes do not.

    c. That team is good but _____ teams are better.

    d. Those racquets are expensive, but _____ racquet is cheap.

    e. Give me _____ tennis balls.

3. Some adjectives add *more* and *most* to make the comparative and superlative degrees. Finish this table. The first one is done for you.

POSITIVE	COMPARATIVE	SUPERLATIVE
wonderful	more wonderful	most wonderful
agile		
competitive		
spectacular		

4. Some adjectives change completely in the comparative and superlative degrees. Complete the following table.

POSITIVE	COMPARATIVE	SUPERLATIVE
many	more	
bad		
little		least
good		

5. Write two adjectives in the superlative degree to complete this rhyme.

    Jenny is the (bright) _____

    Though Tony thinks he's (good) _____

    Tony's pretty clever,

    But Jenny tops each test.

MORE ACTION

- Make lists of descriptive, possessive, numeral, modal, classifying and demonstrative adjectives. See how many you can find.
  Write one of each in a sentence.

Text Type:

REVIEW

ARTICLES

There are three **articles**, *a, an* and *the*, as in *a* group, *an* exciting book and *the* brother. Articles describe nouns, so they are adjectives of a special kind. *The* is called a *definite article* because it refers to a definite or particular thing as in *the* brother. *A* and *an* are called *indefinite articles* because they do not refer to a definite or particular thing. If you said *a* rabbit, you could mean any rabbit. *An* is used in front of a vowel (a, e, i, o, u) or a silent h as in *an* enemy or *an* hour.

Watership Down

Watership Down *by Richard Adams is an exciting book about the remarkable adventures of a group of rabbits. They are led by Hazel, the clever and very brave brother of Fiver.*

The book is a long one but I found it hard to put down. It is a really gripping story. The author has created an imaginary world of rabbits with a rabbit language. Since reading it, I have never felt the same about rabbits again.

1. This is part of a review of *Watership Down* by Richard Adams. (See Review, p. 84.) Circle all the definite articles and box all the indefinite articles in the review.

2. Fill in the spaces with articles. Write **D** for definite or **I** for indefinite after each one.

   a. _____ rabbits on Watership Down lived in _____ rabbit warren.

   b. They had _____ leader called Hazel and _____ enemy called General Woundwort.

   c. They also had _____ friend called Kehaar who was _____ great gull.

3. Add *a* or *an* in front of each word or phrase.

(Watch out for words with a silent aitch (h).)

_____ argument   _____ heir to the throne

_____ eerie sound   _____ itchy spot

_____ brave rabbit   _____ awful battle

_____ hour before dark   _____ honourable act

_____ wonderful novel   _____ umbrella

4. Fill in the space with definite or indefinite articles. That is, write in *the*, *a* or *an*.

a. _____ novelist, Richard Adams is _____ author of many books.

_____ novel, *Watership Down,* won _____ Carnegie Medal,

_____ honour second to none for _____ children's book.

b. *Watership Down* has been described as _____ exciting book, _____

frightening book, _____ imaginative book, _____ beautiful

book, _____ classic of animal literature . . . and many more things beside.

5. Fill in the articles to finish the titles of these books about real or imaginary animals.

_____ *Plague Dogs* by Richard Adams;

_____ *Bear Called Paddington* by Michael Bond;

_____ *Jungle Book* by Rudyard Kipling;

_____ *Incredible Journey* by Sheila Burnford;

_____ *Dog So Small* by Philippa Pearce;

_____ *Broken Saddle* by James Aldridge;

_____ *Wind in the Willows* by Kenneth Grahame;

_____ *Wolves of Willoughby Chase* by Joan Aiken

MORE ACTION

• Find out the names of other books Richard Adams has written. Borrow them from the library if you can. Above all, read *Watership Down* (or see the film or video).
• Write your own review of *Watership Down*, or another of Richard Adam's books, or of a book you have read recently.
• Read as many of the books listed in Exercise 5 as you can. (You may have read some of them before.) Find other books, fiction and non-fiction, that are about animals. Read them too.

TAKE A TEST 1

REVISION: UNITS 1 – 7

1. Fill in the spaces.

a. A noun is the _____ of a person, place or thing.

b. A _____ noun is the name of a special place or thing.

c. A collective noun is the name of a _____ of things.

2. Write down all the common, proper and collective nouns you can find in these sentences. Write them in the correct boxes.
  • Dubbo has a zoo that contains a herd of elephants.
  • Jan saw a flock of gulls.
  • Maria watched a pod of whales in the ocean.

COMMON	PROPER	COLLECTIVE

3. Fill in the spaces.

An _____ noun exists in the mind. You cannot actually touch it.

4. a. Which noun is out of place in these words.

Pedro, Australia, happiness, Peru, New Zealand._____

b. It is an _____ noun.

5. Write **S** for singular or **P** for plural beside each of these nouns.

a. animals _____ ; b. bulls _____ ; c. earth _____ ;

d. mammals _____ ; e. platypus _____ ; f. sheep _____ .

6. Make these nouns plural.

berry _____   leaf _____

monkey _____   fly _____

sheep _____   goose _____

7. Write the feminine gender form of these words.

a. stallion _____   d. gander _____

b. ram _____   e. lion _____

c. boar _____   f. rabbit _____

8. Write two descriptive adjectives, two numeral adjectives and two possessive adjectives from these phrases.

three big pies   my two pets   their kind friends

DESCRIPTIVE	NUMERAL	POSSESSIVE

9. a. Write two classifying adjectives and two modal adjectives from these phrases.

Australian animals,   a slight cold,   a certain win,   library books.

Classifying _____   _____

Modal   _____   _____

b. Write **T** for true or **F** for false in the box after this statement:

A classifying adjective cannot take "very" in front of it. ☐

10. Fill in the spaces to show each degree of these adjectives.

good		
	faster	
many	more	

11. Write **T** for true and **F** for false in the box after the following sentences.

a. The word "the" is a definite article because it refers to a definite thing. ☐

b. The words "a" and "an" are indefinite articles. ☐

NONE WRONG (excellent) ☐	1-2 WRONG (good) ☐	3-4 WRONG (pass) ☐	5 OR MORE WRONG (more work needed) ☐

Text Type:

FACTUAL DESCRIPTION

PRONOUNS: PERSONAL, POSSESSIVE

A **pronoun** is a word that is used in place of a noun. For example, in the sentences, Ben is a beagle. *He* is *mine*. *He* and *mine* are pronouns. A **personal pronoun** is used instead of a person or thing. The personal pronouns are *I, me, he, him, she, her, it, we, us, you, they, them*. A **possessive pronoun** is used in place of a noun and shows ownership, as in He is *mine*. The possessive pronouns are *his, hers, mine, its, ours, yours, theirs*.

Possessive pronouns are different from possessive adjectives, which are always followed by a noun, as in *my* dog.

My Dog, Ben

Ben is a beagle. He is mine. His coat has patches of black, brown and white, so he is called a tri-colour. Beagles are described as scent hounds and Ben is no exception. When I take him for a walk, he sniffs everything within reach. There is no nose like his.

Ben is a gentle and affectionate dog and I have trained him to walk well on a lead. He is very fond of food, so I have to watch his diet. He has a wonderful voice and it can be heard a long way in the distance. I wish I could describe it for you . . .

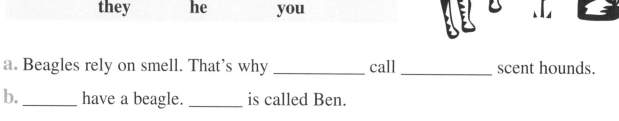

1. Read through the factual description, *My Dog, Ben.* (See Factual Description p. 86.)

   a. Circle all the personal pronouns.

   b. Draw boxes around the two possessive pronouns.

2. Write personal pronouns in the spaces. Pick from the box.

we	him	I	me	them
they		he	you	

   a. Beagles rely on smell. That's why _____ call _____ scent hounds.

   b. _____ have a beagle. _____ is called Ben.

   c. ___ like _____ and _____ likes _____.

   d. _____ should have a beagle for a pet. _____ are affectionate and gentle animals.

3. Colour the boxes that contain possessive pronouns.

she	they	mine	your
my	their	you	our
I	ours	we	yours
hers	them	theirs	its

4. Cross out the underlined words and write a personal pronoun beside it in the space.

a. I own Ben. <u>Ben</u> _____ is my dog.

b. Dogs make good pets. <u>Dogs</u> _____ are faithful animals.

c. Maria and I play with Ben. <u>Maria</u> _____ and I play with Ben.

d. We have a dog and a cat. <u>The dog and the cat</u> _____ are good friends.

e. When Ben was a puppy <u>Ben</u> _____ was playful. His mother fed him. <u>His mother</u> _____ had five pups.

5. Cross out the wrong personal pronoun.

a. (Her, She) and I went walking.

b. She came with Ben and (I, me).

c. You and (I, me) have dogs for pets.

d. He talked to him and (I, me).

e. Sally saw Lisa and (youse, you).

MORE ACTION

• Find out about hounds, especially beagles. What other hounds are there? Write a factual description of a pet dog or cat in your own book or folder. Circle all the personal and possessive pronouns.

• Why are pronouns useful words? Exercise 4 will give you a hint.

PRONOUNS: RELATIVE, INTERROGATIVE, DEMONSTRATIVE

Relative pronouns take the place of nouns and join sentences, as in This is the game *that* I like best. The main relative pronouns are *who, whom, which* and *that.*

Interrogative pronouns ask questions as in *Who* agrees with me? These are often called "wh-" questions and the pronouns are often called question pronouns. Other interrogative pronouns are *what, whom, whose* and *which.*

Demonstrative pronouns stand for nouns and point them out, as in *This* is the best game. Other demonstrative pronouns are *that, those* and *these.*

Note that words like *what* or *that* are interrogative or demonstrative adjectives if they are followed by a noun as in *What* game is best, or *That* game is best.

The Best Sports

Some people think tennis is the best sport. People who play tennis can play it for most of their lives. That is a good thing. Also, tennis is a friendly, social game that everyone can enjoy. It is less dangerous than other sports. This is a good thing, too. Who wants to have a serious injury?

Other people prefer games like basketball, netball, soccer, rugby or cricket, which have many more players who can take part. These are real team games. What could be better? Who could disagree?

1. There are ten pronouns in boxes in the discussion, *The Best Sports.* (See Discussion, p. 85.) Write each one in the correct columns below. Write the word that follows the pronoun also. The first one is done for you.

RELATIVE	INTERROGATIVE	DEMONSTRATIVE
who play		

2. Fill in the spaces with relative pronouns from the box.

who   **which**   **that**   **whom**

(*Who* is nominative case and *whom* is objective case. (See Unit 11).)

a. She is a girl _____ plays cricket.

b. I caught the ball _____ the batsman hit.

c. Sport, _____ is good for you, should be played by everyone.

d. He is the player to _____ I threw the ball.

e. The students, _____ represented the school, went to the Sports Carnival.

f. These are the players _____ I saw.

3. Fill in the interrogative pronouns. Pick from the box.

Which   **whom**   **Who**   **Whose**   **What**

a. _____ plays basketball?

b. _____ are these gym boots?

c. _____ would you prefer?

d. _____ is your favourite sport?

e. To _____ did you write?

4. Fill in the demonstrative pronouns. Pick from the box.

These   **This**   **Those**   **That**

a. _____ is our team in the blue singlets.

b. _____ are our players.

c. _____, over there, are our opposition.

d. _____ is our captain; I'd like you to meet her.

e. _____ are the sports that we think are best.

MORE ACTION

• Think of other arguments for or against the sports in the discussion. Write them down in your own book or folder. Underline the relative, interrogative and demonstrative pronouns you used.

• Have a debate about your favourite sport.
 Use as many pronouns as you can.

Text Type:

NARRATIVE

PRONOUNS: PERSON, NUMBER, GENDER

PERSON

First person is used if we are talking about ourselves (person speaking) as in *I* yelled; **second person** is used if we are talking to someone (person spoken to) as in *You* replied; and **third person** is used if we are talking about someone (person spoken about) as in *They* jumped.

NUMBER

Singular number refers to one thing, as in *She* swam; **plural number** refers to more than one thing, as in *They* swam.

GENDER

Masculine gender refers to a male person or thing, as in *He* is … ; **feminine gender** refers to a female person or thing, as in *She* is … ; and **neuter gender** refers to a thing that is neither male nor female, as in *water* rushed … Often the gender of a pronoun depends on what the text is about or, if it is not clear, it can be called **common gender**, as in animals swam for safety: *They* swam … or can also be termed **masculine** or **feminine gender.**

Flood

    Ka Li fixed his eyes on the surge of yellow water as it rushed towards him. Bobbing on its surface he could see the black hair of his sister, Lu Sing. She was being carried relentlessly forward on the foam-edged crests of the torrent, and was struggling to stay afloat. He had to save her, some way, before she was swept past him and over the waterfall to certain death on the rocks beneath.

    Ka Li had climbed out on one of the branches of a big tree that grew over the water; the river was just below him and he could reach down to it while holding on like a leech with his legs and one arm.

    "Lu Sing!" he yelled as the bobbing head raced towards him.

    "I am here. Ka Li. Grab my hand … Grab my hand!" The little girl raised her arm acknowledging his cry as she sped towards the tree. . .

1. a. Find these personal pronouns in the story. (See Narrative, p. 83.) Highlight, circle or underline them each time they appear.

    b. Now complete this table. The first one is done for you.

he
she
him
her
it

PRONOUN	PERSON	NUMBER	GENDER
I	1st	singular	masculine
he			
she			
her			
him			
it			

2. Here is a useful table that shows you the personal pronouns, their person and number.

	SINGULAR	PLURAL	SINGULAR	PLURAL
lst person	I	we	me	us
2nd person	you	you	you	you
3rd person	he, she, it	they	him, her, it	them

a. Colour the personal pronouns in the table this way:

(i) 3rd person, plural number, red.   (iii) 3rd person, singular number, green.

(ii) 1st person, singular number, blue. (iv) 2nd person, singular number, yellow.

b. Write down the pronouns that are feminine gender. _____

3. Finish these sentences using the correct personal pronouns.

a. (i) Ka Li was brave. _____ saved Lu Sing. _____ was brave, too.

(ii) I was worried about the children. _____ thought the river would

be the end of _____.   (iii) What did _____ think?

b.   Write the person, number and gender of the pronouns in (i), (ii) and (iii).

(i) _____

(ii) _____

(iii) _____

MORE ACTION

• *Flood* is part of an adventure story about two children who escaped from a terrible
flood that devastated their land and drowned many people. Write your own story
about a real or imagined adventure. (See Narrative, p. 83.) Underline all
the personal pronouns in your first page. You will be amazed
how many there are.

PRONOUNS: CASE

Personal and possessive pronouns have **case**. Case can be **nominative, objective** or **possessive**. If a personal pronoun is the subject of a verb it is said to be in the nominative case, as in *He* had to save her. You find the subject of a verb by asking who? or what? in front of it. For example, the verb is "had to save". Who had to save? Answer, "He".

If a personal pronoun is the object of a verb, it is said to be in the objective case, as in He had to save *her*. You find the object of the verb by asking Who? or What? after it, for example, the verb is "had to save". Had to save who or what? Answer, "her".

A pronoun is in the objective case if it is the object of a preposition, as in towards *him*.

Possessive pronouns are said to be in the possessive case, because they show ownership, as in *her* fingers or *his*.

Flood (continued)

"*Now!*" *he shouted, as the little girl swept under him. "Now!"*

He grabbed for the outstretched arm and felt the cold, small fingers clench on his. For a split second his grip seemed to be slipping ... and then – and then it held. The raging river seemed cheated and tugged at Lu Sing's body. Her weight felt unbearable to Ka Li and his grip on the tree was tested to breaking point. One slip and they would both be gone.

But slowly, so slowly, Ka Li began to pull the little girl up, out of the water. Every centimetre he lifted her, she seemed to become lighter as the relentless tug of the river lessened. Then with a final burst of energy Ka Li dragged Lu Sing onto the branch. The two children hugged each other, faces pressed together. His to hers and hers to his. They were both weeping, not with grief but with joy. They were safe.

1. Find these possessive pronouns in the narrative: *his* and *hers*. (See Narrative, p. 83.) Highlight, circle or underline them each time they appear.

PERSONAL AND POSSESSIVE PRONOUNS

PERSONAL PRONOUNS				
	NOMINATIVE CASE		OBJECTIVE CASE	
	SINGULAR	PLURAL	SINGULAR	PLURAL
1st person	I	we	me	us
2nd person	you	you	you	you
3rd person	he, she, it	they	him, her, it	them

POSSESSIVE PRONOUNS		
	POSSESSIVE CASE	
	SINGULAR	PLURAL
1st person	mine	ours
2nd person	yours	yours
3rd person	his, hers, its	theirs

2. These useful tables show you all the personal and possessive pronouns as well as their person, number and case.

a. Colour the boxes in the table which show:

(i) the pronoun that is 1st person, singular number, possessive case. (Red)

(ii) the pronoun that is 3rd person, plural number, objective case. (Green)

(iii) the pronouns that are 3rd person, singular number, nominative case. (Blue)

b. Finish these sentences with the correct pronouns.

(i) This story is mine. That story is _____ (2nd person, singular, possessive case).

(ii) He was able to save _____ (3rd person, singular, objective case).

(iii) I was pleased for _____ (3rd person, plural, objective case).

(iv) _____ were both safe (3rd person, plural, nominative case).

(v) He grabbed her hand with _____ (3rd person, singular, possessive case).

MORE ACTION

• Imagine that you were the author of this adventure story. (See Narrative, p. 83.) Write what happened next. (The children had to find food, the land was flooded, they were lost, they saw a big snake . . .) Underline the personal and possessive pronouns in your first page.

UNIT 12

VERBS: ACTION, SAYING, THINKING, RELATING

Verbs are doing, being and having words, as in I *jump*, I *am* happy and I *have* a friend.

We can give verbs extra names to describe them more fully, such as **action verbs** (dart, dash, jump), **saying verbs** (said, yelled), **thinking verbs** (thought, considered) and **relating verbs** (am, have, become.)

Me – Moving

I dart and dash,
I jig and jump,
I scamper,
Skate and scramble.
I strut and stride,
I slip and slide,
And frequently, I amble.

I leap and lurch,
I crawl and creep,
I rove and romp and ramble.
I turn and trip,
I skid and skip,
And now and then –
I gambol!

1. This poem is full of action words. (See Poetry, p. 84.)

   a. Highlight, underline or circle each one.

   b. Find the exact meaning of *scramble, amble, ramble* and *gambol* in your dictionary. Write the meanings of these words in your own book or folder.

   c. What other "moving" words can you think of? Use your thesaurus to help you. Write them in your book, also.

2. Write interesting *saying verbs* to fill the spaces.

   a. "You are hurting my toe," I _____.

   b. "Run! Run!" I _____.

c. "I still have to think about that," I _____ in a slow voice.

d. "That is my lunch," I _____ angrily.

e. "Could I have a turn, now," I _____ politely.

3. Write interesting *thinking verbs* to fill these spaces. Pick from the box or use others.

considered   consider   debated   believe   Think   contemplate

a. It is something we would have to _____.

b. _____ carefully before you answer this question.

c. Our school _____ against Hilltop Primary. The topic was "Rock music is a passing fad."

d. I firmly _____ that this is the right thing to do.

e. The jury _____ the matter for two hours.

4. Write in the correct parts of the verb "to be" to fill the spaces.

a. I have _____ waiting for an hour.

b. They _____ here yesterday.

c. I _____, you _____, we _____ Australian.

d. Be quiet! We _____ doing our homework.

e. She _____ here a little while ago; I don't know where she _____ now.

5. Write the full form of these contractions. The first one is done for you.

he's _____he is_____   she's _____

you're _____   I've _____

you've _____   they're _____

there's _____   I'm _____

we're _____   they've _____

MORE ACTION

• In your own book or folder, write as many *thinking verbs* as you can find in your thesaurus or have a class "think tank" and write the words on the board.

VERBS: TENSE, VOICE

Verbs have **tense** and **voice**.

There are three tenses, *present, past* and *future*. Present tense refers to actions that are happening now, as in They *are* fearsome predators. *Are* is said to be in the *timeless* present, also, because the action is continuous. Past tense refers to actions that happened in the past, as in They *were hunted*. Future tense refers to actions that will happen in the future, as in they *will eat* . . .

Voice is **active** or **passive**. If the subject is doing the action, the verb is active voice, as in Great White Sharks *are* the giants . . . Here, the verb *are* is active voice because the subject, great white sharks, is the doer. If the verb is passive voice, the subject has something done to it, as in They *were hunted*. *Were hunted* is passive voice because the subject, *they,* has something done to it. Verbs in the passive voice have an auxiliary or helping verb, in this case, *were.*

Great White Sharks

Great White Sharks are the giants of the fish world. They will grow up to six metres in length and will weigh 3,000 kilograms as adults. They are grey or bronze on the back and white underneath. They have a crescent-shaped tail, large dorsal fins and a pointed snout with sharp serrated teeth.

Great Whites are fearsome predators. The juveniles eat squid and other fish but the adults prefer seals, sea lions and dolphins. They will eat humans, also.

These mighty creatures are found in temperate coastal waters, all over the world – but they were hunted severely in the past and their numbers have decreased. Great White Sharks are now protected in Australian waters and other countries have followed this lead.

1. a. Underline or highlight the verbs in the above information report.
   (See Information Report, p. 87.)

   b. Fill in this table with three verbs from the report in each column.

PRESENT	PAST	FUTURE

2. Write the tense of these verbs beside each one.

e. eat _____   f. will continue_____

b. will eat _____   g. decrease _____

c. ate _____   h. followed _____

d. hunted _____   i. grows _____

e. were found _____   j. encountered _____

3. a. In your own book or folder, rewrite the following passage with verbs in the present tense.

b. Then rewrite it with verbs in the future tense.

Great White Sharks were fierce and dangerous creatures. If you swam near them they ate you. They thought you were a seal. They killed for food, not for pleasure.

4. Change these sentences from active to passive voice. The first one is done for you.

a. The Great White Shark eats seals.

Seals are eaten by the Great White Shark.

b. They will eat humans, too.

c. We protect these sharks in our waters.

d. Men caught many Great White Sharks.

e. I have seen a Great White Shark.

MORE ACTION

- Find out more about Great White Sharks. Write another paragraph of the information report. (See Information Report, p. 87.)
- What tense are the verbs in your paragraph? Can you tell why they are in that tense?

Text Type:

PROCEDURE

ADVERBS

Adverbs add meaning to verbs, adjectives and other adverbs, as in: bite *cautiously, very* hot, *too* quickly. Adverbs that say **how** *(cautiously)* are adverbs of **manner**. Adverbs that say **when** *(now)* are adverbs of **time**. Adverbs that say **where** *(down)* are adverbs of place. Other types of adverbs are **interrogative adverbs**. *Where* in *Where* are you going? or *When* in *When* will you arrive?

Modal adverbs express amounts of certainty as in *possibly, probably* and *definitely*. **Negative adverbs** are words such as *not* or *never*.

How to Eat a Hot Meat Pie

Things You Need
- *A piping hot meat pie*
- *Tomato sauce*
- *Soap, water and paper towel (optional)*

What To Do
- *Carefully remove the pie from its bag or other container.*
- *Hold pie firmly in the hand and pour sauce over.*
- *Then bite cautiously into the pastry.*
- *Blow gently on the very hot meat and gravy.*
- *Eat immediately with small bites, but not too quickly as pie will be hot inside.*
- *Suck up any meat or gravy that drips down.*
- *Frequently wipe chin with tissue or paper towel, kept near.*
- *Finally, finish the pie quickly to avoid excess spillage.*
- *Now, wash hands and face thoroughly. (Optional)*

Bon appetit!

1. Underline or highlight the adverbs
in the above procedure.
(See Procedure, p. 88.)

(Note that a number of adverbs end in "ly"– but some don't.)

2. Finish this table with adverbs from the procedure.

MANNER (how)	TIME (when)	PLACE (where)
carefully	Then	over

3. Finish these sentences with an adverb.

a. Eat a hot pie _____ (manner)

b. Don't let it fall _____ (place)   c. Finish your pie _____ (time)

4. Write opposites (antonyms) of these adverbs: *quickly,   down,   inside,   over,   carefully,   finally,   gently,   frequently,   everywhere.*

_____

_____

5. Make adverbs from these adjectives.

hungry _____   greedy _____

careful _____   thorough _____

cautious _____   immediate _____

serious _____   complete _____

occasion _____   polite _____

MORE ACTION

* Write your own procedure entitled *How to Cook Rice* or *How to Make a Super-Delicious Sandwich*. (See Procedure p. 88.)
* Synonyms are words of similar meaning, such as *enormously* and *gigantically*. Find synonyms for the following adverbs: *totally, powerfully, energetically, presently, immediately, loudly, quickly* and *instantly.* Use your thesaurus to help you.

Text Type:

LITERARY DESCRIPTION

PREPOSITIONS

A **preposition** is a word that is placed in front of a noun or pronoun in a prepositional phrase, as in *in* our old car or *to* Brighton. A preposition is related to the noun or pronoun that ends the phrase. *In* is related to car and *to* is related to Brighton. Prepositions are usually little words, like *in, at, of, for, with* or *into*, although some are long, like *below, underneath* or *between*.

1944

My name is Edward (call me Ted) and I live in *Bexley, a suburb of Sydney. Our country is at war and things are tough: no money for toys and very little for food. Clothes are scarce, too, and going out in our old car is a rare thing, because there is petrol rationing in Australia. We have to save for the war effort.*

My favourite pastime is swimming at the baths in Botany Bay or fishing underneath the old pier. My friend Johnny and I ride our bikes to Brighton-le-Sands or run through the stormwater channels to the Bay.

1. This literary description may remind you of *My Place* by Nadia Wheatley and Donna Rawlins. It is like that interesting book because it is a literary description that describes a place, a time and an experience. (See Literary Description, p. 82.)

   a. Read through *1944* and draw boxes around all the prepositions.

   b. Underline or highlight the nouns or pronouns to which they relate.

   c. Draw a bracket from each preposition to its related noun or pronoun. The first one is done for you.

2. Finish these sentences with prepositions. Pick from the box.

among   **beside**   **between**   **besides**   **into**   **in**

a. We shared the fish _____ Johnny and me.

b. We caught so many fish we shared them _____ all the people in our street.

c. We dived _____ the water.

d. We swam _____ the baths.

e. Johnny fished _____ me.

f. There was no one there _____ us.

3. Warning! Watch out for adverbs!

If words like *after, down* or *past* have no noun following, they are adverbs as in

He walked *past.*

Underline the adverb or preposition and write "preposition" or "adverb" in each space.

a. I fell down. _____

b. We ran down the stormwater drain. _____

c. We walked along the pier. _____

d. Come along! _____

e. The bike went past. _____

f. The bus went past the door. _____

MORE ACTION

- Photocopy a page of the book you are reading. Underline all the prepositions you can find.
- Select a year in your life and write a literary description, like *1944.* Underline the prepositions in it.
- There are many prepositions that are not used in this unit. Find as many new ones as you can and write them in a sentence.

Text Type:

FACTUAL RECOUNT

CONJUNCTIONS: CO-ORDINATE AND SUBORDINATE

Conjunctions are joining words. They join words, groups of words, and sentences, as in Dad *and* I, The course was very long *and* very difficult. Karrie Webb played well, *but* she did not win.

And and *but* are **co-ordinate conjunctions**. They join similar and equal things. **Subordinate conjunctions** join unequal parts of sentences. One part (clause) is subordinate to or dependent on another. The subordinate clause cannot stand alone, as in We needed drinks *because* it was a hot day. *Because* is the subordinate conjunction and *because it was a hot day* is the subordinate clause that cannot stand alone.

Watching the Golf

On Sunday, Dad and I went to see the final day of the Australian Women's Open Golf Championship. It was a big event and I was very excited. I like netball, but I really like golf, too. We went to the parking lot when we arrived and caught the shuttle bus to Terrey Hills Golf Club. We had a backpack with our sandwiches and drinks. We needed drinks because it was a very warm day.

Dad and I followed different players after everyone had hit off. You could stand quite near them and watch. The course was long and very difficult I thought but the players did not seem to worry as they can hit the ball so far and so straight.

Mhairy McKay from Scotland won, although the result was close. She was one stroke ahead of Laura Davies from England. Our Karrie Webb played well but she did not win. They are all great players and interesting people, too.

1. **a.** Circle each example of a co-ordinate conjunction in the factual recount. (See Factual Recount, p. 87.)

    b. Underline each part a co-ordinate conjunction joins, like this *Dad* and *I*.

    c. Find the following subordinate conjunctions in the factual recount and draw boxes around them.

        when   **because**   **after**   **as**   **although**

    d. Underline the clause each one begins.

2. Use a coordinate conjunction to join the following.

a. I like golf _____ I don't play much.

b. I play tennis _____ netball.

c. They all played well _____ there was only one winner.

d. We ate our lunch _____ felt refreshed.

e. You can watch _____ you must be quiet.

3. Use subordinate conjunctions to finish these sentences. Pick from the box.

> **When**   **after**   **if**   **because**   **when**

a. She won _____ she played so well.

b. We had a pizza _____ the championship finished.

c. You will be in trouble_____ you move _____ the players are hitting.

d. _____ I go out with Dad I have fun.

4. Write three sentences, each containing one of these subordinate conjunctions.
In your own book or folder, write sentences that contain the others:

| although | unless | because | when | while |
| before | whether | after | neither … nor | either … or. |

(Remember that they must be part of a clause. (See Clauses, Unit 21.))

a. _____

_____

b. _____

_____

c. _____

_____

MORE ACTION

• Write a factual recount of your experiences at a sporting event, movie, picnic
or bush walk. Circle all the co-ordinate conjunctions and make boxes
around the subordinate conjunctions you have used.

REVISION: UNITS 8 – 16

1. Complete these sentences.

A pronoun is a word that is used_____

A _____ pronoun shows ownership.

2. Circle the pronouns in these sentences. Write them in your own book or folder and print PERSONAL or POSSESSIVE after each one.

It is mine.   He is ours.   They are theirs.

We ate ours.   Did you eat yours.

3. Circle the pronouns in these sentences. Write them in your own book or folder and print RELATIVE, INTERROGATIVE or DEMONSTRATIVE after each one.

That is the girl who won the prize.   What is the answer?

Whom did you see?   This is mine.   Whose are these?

Those are the students whom I saw.

4. Write the following pronouns in your own book or folder: *she, him, it* and *we,* then write the person, number and gender after each one.

5. Write personal or possessive after these pronouns.

a. I _____   c. mine _____

b. theirs _____   d. her _____

6. Write the case of the pronouns in the boxes.

a. I saw her. She was with them.   b. The book was theirs, not ours.

I _____   her _____

She _____   them _____

theirs _____   ours _____

7. State the type of verb in each case. Write action, saying, thinking or relating.

a. jumped _____   c. shouted _____

b. thought _____   d. was _____

8. Write the tense of these verbs. Write present, past or future.

a. eats _____   c. ate _____

b. will eat _____   d. went _____

9. State if the underlined verbs are in the active or passive voice.

a. The shark <u>ate</u> the seal.   _____

b. The seal <u>was eaten</u> by a shark.   _____

10. Write the type of adverb in each case. Write manner, time or place.

I walked slowly.   I fell down.   I arrived early.

slowly _____   down _____   early _____

11. Write preposition or adverb after each boxed word.

He jumped |into| _____ the water, swam |across| _____

the lake and watched the boats go |past|. _____

12. Underline the co-ordinate conjunctions and draw boxes around the subordinate conjunctions.

I saw the movie and ate some popcorn because I was hungry. I went home when the

show was finished but I would like to see it again.

Text Type:

REVIEW

NOUN GROUP

A **noun group** is a group of words providing information about people, places and things in sentences. It is based on a head word as in *a very nasty bully*. In this noun group the head word is *bully*.

Sometimes a noun group consists of only one noun or pronoun, as in taking *presents* or *she* is eventually caught.

At other times a noun group can be much longer, as in *her two equally nasty friends,* or it can have more words after the head word, as in *a novel about bullies. About bullies* is called a **post modifier**. A noun group is also called a **noun phrase** or a **nominal group**.

The Present Takers

The Present Takers *by Aidan Chambers is a book about a very nasty bully named Melanie and her two equally nasty friends. Melanie's main victim in this novel is Lucy Hall who is supported by her good friend, Angus Burns.*

Melanie's victimisation includes taking presents from other students' and hurting them. She is eventually caught out trying to make Lucy steal from a shop. Her final exposure appears in the class newspaper with a series of entries, entitled Guess Who?

This is a really exciting novel as it tells a good story and the writer shows us ways of dealing with people like Melanie Prosser.

1. Complete the following noun groups from the above review. (See Review, p. 84.)

   a. The Present _____ _____ _____ Chambers

   b. her _____ _____ _____ friends

   c. Melanie's main _____ _____ _____ novel

   d. her final _____ _____ _____ _____ newspaper

   e. a really _____ novel.

2. Underline or highlight the noun groups in the following sentences.

a. This novel about bullies is an exciting piece of writing.

b. She was a cruel and unfeeling person.

c. Angus Burns was a true friend in every way.

d. Lucy's parents were kind and understanding people.

e. The class newspaper exposed this unpleasant school bully.

3. Build these noun groups with words from the boxes.

a.   **unfeeling**   **an**   **school**   **a**

_____ bully,   _____ _____ bully,

_____ _____ , _____ bully.

b.   **well thought-out**   **a**   **clever**

___ plan,   ___ _____ plan,

___ _____ , _____ plan.

4. Write descriptive adjectives to finish these noun groups.

a / an _____ novel

a / an _____ _____ novel

a / an _____ _____ novel about

_____ bullies.

5. Underline or highlight the long noun groups in these sentences.

a. A well-written exciting novel for older students must have an interesting and well-developed plot.

b. The characters in an interesting novel for older students must be well-drawn, realistic and recognisable people.

MORE ACTION

• Build your own noun groups about characters in a novel you have read.
• Write your own review of a novel you have read recently. (See Review, p. 84.)

Text Type:

LITERARY RECOUNT

VERB GROUP

The **verb group** of words is based on a main verb (head word) as in *had been **crushed***. In this verb group, the main verb or head word is *crushed*. The other words are helping verbs, also called **auxiliary verbs**. Sometimes the verb group consists of only one word, as in *knew*.

Shackleton's Remarkable Voyage

Now that the Endurance *had been crushed by ice, Shackleton knew that there was only one course of action. He must sail from Elephant Island in Antarctica to South Georgia – a distance of 800 miles (1,288 kilometres). This must be done across a wild ocean, lashed by unceasing gales and battered by raging seas.*

The voyage would have to be undertaken in a semi-open boat, the James Caird, *22 feet (under seven metres) in length with five other men. Navigation would be difficult as sightings with the sextant would be few. If Frank Worsley made a mistake with direction, the men on board would certainly perish and the 27 others, stranded on Elephant Island, would never be rescued ...*

1. Finish these incomplete verb groups from the above literary recount. (See Literary Recount, p. 82.)

   a. had _____ crushed

   b. _____ sail

   c. must _____ done

   d. would _____ to _____ _____

   e. would _____ _____ rescued.

2. Now underline or highlight all the verb groups, including those in Exercise 1.

3. Use auxiliary verbs from the box to finish these sentences.

was   have   will   had   will   were

a. They _____ sailing in perilous seas.

b. The *Endurance* _____ crushed by ice.

c. Shackleton's voyage _____ never be forgotten.

d. They would _____ missed South Georgia if Frank Worsley,

the navigator, _____ made a mistake.

e. I _____ never forget seeing the film on Shackleton's expedition.

4.

Participles are parts of verbs ending in "ing" (present participles) or "ed" (past participles) (when the verb is regular). They are used with auxiliaries to form verb groups.

Finish this table.

PRESENT		PAST	
He is sailing.		He had	.
They	sailing.	They	sailed.
He	doing.	He had	.
They	doing.	They	done.

5. Finish these sentences with past participles.

a. They had (sail) _____ 800 miles (1,288 kilometres).

b. The *Endurance* was (crush) _____ by ice.

c. Gales had (lash) _____ the little boat.

MORE ACTION

• Find out more about Shackleton's remarkable expedition of 1914-1916.
  Write two paragraphs to continue this literary recount.
  (See Literary Recount, p. 82.) Underline the verb groups.

Text Type:

PROCEDURE

PREPOSITIONAL PHRASES: ADVERBIAL, ADJECTIVAL

A **prepositional phrase** consists of a preposition, such as *in, on, with* and *from*, followed by a noun group. Examples are *with a long handle* and *in the ground*. Prepositional phrases have no finite verb (a verb with a subject).

Adverbial prepositional phrases are adverbials. They do the work of adverbs as in Cover *with mulch*. *With mulch* adds meaning to (modifies) the verb, *cover*. Adverbial phrases, like adverbs, tell HOW, WHEN, WHERE and WHY.

Adjectival prepositional phrases, like adjectives, tell us more about (describe) nouns or pronouns, as in A young tree *in a pot*. *In a pot* describes the tree. Which tree? The tree in a pot. We need to be careful to separate adverbial phrases from adjectival phrases. Remember, adjectival phrases add meaning to nouns and they are usually near them, but be careful! Adverbial phrases can be near nouns also, as in Place the young tree *in the hole*. *In the hole* tells where the young tree is placed. It is an adverbial phrase.

How to Plant a Tree

You will need
- *A young tree in a pot*
- *A small amount of fertiliser from a shop*
- *A bag of horse or cow manure*
- *Mulch (leaves, straw, wood chip) to spread on the ground*
- *A spade with a long handle*
- *A hose*

Method
- *Find a suitable place.*
- *Dig in the ground to make a large hole.*
- *Pour a handful of fertiliser in the hole and add some soil.*
- *Pour some water into the hole.*
- *Remove the young tree from the pot.*
- *Place the young tree in the hole.*
- *Fill with soil.*
- *Make a dish shape to save water.*
- *Spread manure around the tree.*
- *Cover top with mulch.*
- *Water the tree lightly with the hose.*

Watch it grow!

1. Circle the prepositions in both parts of this procedure, then underline the phrases they begin. (See Procedure, p. 88.)

2. Write **adj.** (for adjective) or **adv.** (for adverb) on the top of each phrase.

3. Write **adj.** or **adv.** beside each underlined phrase.

a. Dig in the ground _____

b. Cover with mulch_____

c. Water around the tree _____

d. a garden of trees _____

e. a shovel with a long handle _____

f. a tree near a tap _____

g. a bag of cow manure _____

h. Place it in the hole _____

i. Cover with leaves _____

j. a hole in the ground _____

4. Underline the adverbial phrase in this short verse. Circle the verb it modifies.

> *Roots underneath*
>
> *a tree are spread*
>
> *to hold it up*
>
> *and keep it fed.*

5. Underline all the phrases in these noun groups. Finish this sentence.

They are all _____ phrases. Say why in the box.

a. a tree in the meadow

b. a flower on a tree

c. a cow in the pasture

d. a forest of trees

e. the trees beside the river

MORE ACTION

- Write your own procedure describing *How to Walk the Dog,*
  How to Play My Favourite Sport or *How to Make a Sandwich.* (See Procedure, p. 88.)
- Underline all the phrases in your procedure. Which ones are adjectival phrases?
  Which ones are adverbial phrases?

Text Type:

DISCUSSION

SENTENCES:
STATEMENT, QUESTION, EXCLAMATION, COMMAND

A **sentence** is a group of words that makes sense by itself. It is a complete idea. Every sentence starts with a capital letter and ends with a full stop, question mark or exclamation mark. A sentence that ends with a full stop is called a **statement**, as in *Roads provide for many different types of transport.* A sentence that ends with a question mark is a **question**, as in *Don't you agree?*, and a sentence that ends in an exclamation mark is called an **exclamation,** as in *This must be better!* A **command**, such as *Drive safely.* or *Jump out of the way!* can end with either a full stop or an exclamation mark.

More Roads or More Railways 1

There are two sides to this argument. People who support more roads say that trains can only follow rail tracks and are limited. Roads allow the users to take many different routes. Again, railways would never be built where many roads go. Roads open up the country and allow expansion.

Roads are more convenient to use, also. People do not have to follow timetables or wait at stations if they use roads. They provide for many different types of transport, too. Cars, buses, trucks, bicycles, and even pedestrians, can use roads. This must be better! Don't you agree?

1. a. How many sentences are there in this part of a discussion. (See Discussion, p. 85.)

    Write the number in the box. ☐

    b. Write the question and the exclamation on the lines below.

    Question _____

    Exclamation _____

2. Combine the following short sentences to make a longer sentence in each case. The first one is done for you.

    a. Roads provide for flexible use. Roads do not need rail tracks.

    Roads provide for flexible use because they do not need rail tracks.

b. You can use a bicycle, bus, car or truck. You travel on a road.

_____

_____

c. Roads are built in the country. Roads open up the country areas.

_____

_____

d. Roads are easier to use. You don't have to wait on stations. You don't have to "follow" timetables.

_____

_____

_____

3. Finish these sentences with your own ideas.

a. Roads are convenient because _____

_____

b. Roads provide for many _____

_____

c. Roads allow users to _____

_____

4. Put the correct stops in the boxes at the ends of these sentences.

a. Roads are convenient to use ☐   d. May I drive now ☐

b. Look out for that car ☐   e. Please close the bus door, driver ☐

c. Do you prefer roads or railways ☐

MORE ACTION

• Can you think of more reasons why roads are important? Write them in your own book or folder. (See Discussion, p. 85.)

• Finish these sentences in your own book or folder.
Roads are important because . . .
Roads do not need . . .
If you live in the country . . .
When you do not live near a railway station . . .
Look out for . . .

CLAUSES: PRINCIPAL AND SUBORDINATE

A **clause** is a group of words that contains a **finite verb** and its **subject**. When a verb has a subject it is called a finite verb, as in *Trains **are** more environmentally friendly.*

A **principal clause** always makes sense by itself, as in the sentence above, beginning *Trains are …* Every sentence must contain at least one principal clause and sometimes a principal clause is a sentence by itself as in *Trains are environmentally friendly.*

A **subordinate** (dependent) **clause** does not make sense by itself, as in *that are of vital importance.* A subordinate clause adds meaning to a sentence and does the work of an adjective, adverb or noun.

More Roads or More Railways 2

Other people argue that we <u>need</u> more railways. Trains are more environmentally friendly. They <u>produce</u> less greenhouse gas emissions and one train <u>can carry</u> many more people than one car.

Also, trains do not clog up the streets of capital cities. In the country they <u>do not cause</u> the destruction of tracts of trees, which <u>are</u> of vital importance to Australia. Well, what is the answer? Maybe we <u>need</u> more roads and more railways, because our population <u>is growing</u>. A suitable mix, which is carefully planned, <u>could give</u> us the best of both worlds.

To find the subject of a verb you ask Who? or What? in front of it, as in *Other people argue.* Question: Who argue? Answer: Other people, so *Other people* is the subject and *argue* is the finite verb.

1. Find the subjects of the underlined verbs in Discussion 2. Write them here.

_____

_____

2. Write PRINCIPAL or SUBORDINATE beside each of these clauses.

a. Other people argue _____

b. that we need more railways _____

c. Trains are more environmentally friendly _____

d. because our population is growing _____

e. which is carefully planned _____

f. A suitable mix could give us the best of both worlds _____

3. Join each principal clause to the correct subordinate clause. In some cases you will be able to join a principal clause to more than one subordinate clause. The first one is done for you.

Trains are needed   that help reduce erosion.

Other people argue   who were building the railway.

Don't cut down the trees   because they cause less pollution.

We saw the men   that we need more railways.

We will need more railways   when our population grows.

4. Make the verbs agree with their subject in these principal clauses. Cross out the wrong words.

a. Trees (is, are) important.

b. Railways (has, have) an important role to play.

c. Railways and roads (is, are) both needed.

d. He is one of the men who (believe, believes) in railways.

e. Roads that pass through many country towns (is, are) being built.

5. Here are three subordinate clauses from Discussion 2. Write NOUN CLAUSE, ADJECTIVAL CLAUSE or ADVERBIAL CLAUSE beside each one.

a. because our population is growing _____

b. that we need more railways _____

c. which are of vital importance to Australia _____

MORE ACTION

- In your own book, add these types of clauses to each of the following:
  More railways (finish the principal clause)
  Railways are needed because (adverbial clause of reason)
  Roads and railways are needed when (adverbial clause of time)
  People who (adjectival clause) do not care about the environment.
- Can you think of more reasons railways are important?
  Write them in your book. (See Discussion, p. 85.)

Text Type:

FACTUAL RECOUNT

CLAUSES: DIRECT AND INDIRECT OBJECT; THEME AND RHEME

A **clause** can have a **direct object**, i.e. a noun group or pronoun after the verb. In the clause, Emily loved *that story*, *that story* is the **direct object** of the verb *loved*. To find the direct object you ask Who? or What? after the finite verb. QUESTION: loved what? ANSWER: *that story*. A clause can have a **direct** and **indirect object**, also. The indirect object usually has a preposition in front of it, as in Emily used to give the book to *me*. The preposition can be omitted, as in I used to read *Emily* a story ... Here, *Emily* is the indirect object and a *story* is the direct object.

The **theme** of a clause is its first part, as in *I* used to read Emily a story. It can be the subject, but this is not always the case.

The **rheme** is the remainder of the clause, as in I *used to read Emily a story.* The way a clause begins has an effect on its meaning. It places emphasis on certain parts of a clause, as in *Again and again* I would read it. Varying the theme is very important in your writing.

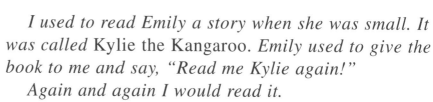

I used to read Emily a story when she was small. It was called Kylie the Kangaroo. *Emily used to give the book to me and say, "Read me Kylie again!"*

Again and again I would read it.

The story was about a tiny kangaroo who lived before kangaroos hopped. Kylie learned to hop when she was bitten by bull-ants. (Being bitten by bull-ants would make anyone hop.) She then taught all the other kangaroos in Australia to hop, and they have been hopping ever since.

Emily loved that story.

1. Underline or highlight the direct objects in the following clauses.

   a. I used to read Emily a story.

   b. It was called *Kylie the Kangaroo*.

   c. Again and again I would read it.

   d. Emily used to give the book to me.

   e. She then taught all the other kangaroos in Australia to hop.

2. Underline or highlight the indirect objects.

a. I used to read Emily a story.

b. Emily used to give me the book.

c. Read me Kylie again!

d. Read her that book, please.

e. I read the book to her.

3. Draw a box around the theme in each sentence and underline or highlight the rheme.

a. It was called *Kylie the Kangaroo.*

b. Being bitten by a bull-ant would make anyone hop.

c. Again and again I would read it.

d. Emily loved that story.

e. That story was loved by Emily.

4. Passive voice changes the theme and the emphasis in a clause. (See Passive Voice, Unit 13.) Write these clauses, that happen to be sentences also, into passive form. The first one is done for you.

a. I read the book to Emily.   The book was read to Emily by me.

b. The bull-ants bit Kylie.

c. She taught other kangaroos to hop.

d. Emily loved that story.

e. I liked the story, too.

MORE ACTION

• If you have read a story to a small brother or sister ... or maybe another child, write a factual recount of your experience. (See Factual Recount, p. 87.) Vary the theme in your sentences as much as you can.   OR   Write a factual recount of a place you visited with a small child. It may or may not have been a lot of fun!

• In your own book, write some sentences using these formats.

a. SUBJECT – VERB – OBJECT (SVO) as in *Ants bit Kylie.*

b. SUBJECT – VERB – DIRECT OBJECT – INDIRECT OBJECT (S V DO IO) as in *They gave the cakes to me.*

c. SUBJECT – VERB – INDIRECT OBJECT – DIRECT OBJECT (S V IO DO) *She gave them the cakes.*

23 ULURU

SENTENCES: COMPOUND AND COMPLEX

A **compound sentence** combines two or more principal clauses with the co-ordinate conjunctions **and** or **but**, as in *It stands 348 metres above the desert and is 9.4 kilometres around the base.*

A **complex sentence** combines two or more clauses, one being a subordinate clause, as in *Uluru is sacred to the Anangu people who arrived there 30,000 years ago* or *When you visit Uluru, see these natural wonders . . .* Some complex sentences can have more than one principal clause. They are sometimes called compound/complex sentences.

Uluru

Uluru is a gigantic rocky outcrop in the Red Centre of Australia. It stands 348 metres above the desert and is 9.4 kilometres around the base. Its deep red colour is caused by iron oxide in the sandstone (arkose) that was compressed and pushed up by natural forces about 400 million years ago.

Uluru is sacred to the Anangu people who arrived there 30,000 years before us. It was returned to them in 1985 as part of the Uluru-Kata Tjuta National Park which measures 1,325 square kilometres.

When you visit the centre of Australia, see this magnificent natural wonder because it is truly unique.

1. Add another principal clause to each of the following to make a compound sentence. Remember that each principal clause must have a finite verb.

   a. Uluru is in the Red Centre of Australia and

   _____.

   b. The rock is red in colour and

   _____.

   c. Uluru is made of sandstone and

   _____.

   d. It may take a long while to fly or drive to Uluru but

   _____

2. Join the principal clauses to make compound sentences. Write in your own book or folder.

You are permitted to climb Uluru	and they are the traditional owners.
Uluru is deep red	and it is 9.4 kilometres around the base.
Uluru is sacred to the aboriginal people	but the Anangu do not like you to do it.
The Rock is 348 metres high	and it appears to change colour at different times of the day.

> Subordinate clauses in complex sentences make our writing more interesting.
> They also stop us from using too many short sentences joined by "and".

3. Find the clauses in the factual description *Uluru* that begin with the following relative pronouns: *that, who, which*. (See Factual Description, p. 86.) Write the clauses in your own book or folder and say what type of subordinate clause each one is.

4. Fill in the correct answers.

The two subordinate clauses, *When you visit the centre of Australia* and *because it is truly unique* are _____ clauses. The first one is an

_____ clause of _____ and the second

one is an _____ clause of _____ .

5. In your own book or folder, finish these complex sentences with subordinate clauses. The beginnings are supplied. Use your own words.

a. The Anangu are native people who

b. You must see Uluru because

c. Be sure to take photographs when

d. I am sure that

MORE ACTION

- Kata Tjuta is another remarkable spectacle. It is 25 km from Uluru.
  Find out about Kata Tjuta in your library, on the Internet or from a travel agency.
  Write your own factual description of it. (See Factual Description, p. 86.)
  Use as many interesting sentences as you can.

TAKE A TEST 3

REVISION: UNITS 17 - 23

1. Underline the noun groups in these sentences.

a. The novel by Aidan Chambers was an interesting book.

b. The characters in the novel helped to make a good story.

2. Underline the verb groups in these sentences.

a. I have been reading this interesting book.

b. They had told us that they were reading the book.

c. We will have seen the movie by Saturday.

3. Find the prepositional phrases. Write them down in your own book or folder and say if they are adjectival or adverbial.

a. We sat in the library and read the book about trees.

b. Always bring a bag of fertiliser.

c. Walk to the shops and buy a tree in a pot.

4. Write the type of sentence after each of the following. Write **S** for Statement, **Q** for Question, **E** for Exclamation or **C** for Command.

a. He is my friend. _____   c. Where are you going? _____

b. Give me that ball. _____   d. Watch out! _____

5. Write PRINCIPAL or SUBORDINATE beside each of the following clauses:

a. because she is my friend _____

b. Give me that! _____

c. Who was in the pool? _____

d. Where are they? _____

e. which I really enjoyed _____

6. Write NOUN CLAUSE, ADJECTIVAL CLAUSE or ADVERBIAL CLAUSE for each of the underlined clauses.

    a. We need more railways <u>because our population is growing.</u>

    _____

    b. I knew <u>that I could do it.</u> _____

    c. The transport system, <u>which is under stress</u>, needs improvement.

    _____

7. Underline the direct objects and draw boxes around the indirect objects in these sentences.

    a. She gave me a present.   **c.** Give the book to me.

    b. I threw them the ball.   **d.** We read James a story.

8. Highlight or underline the theme in these sentences.

    a. Kylie was a clever kangaroo.   **c.** Always clean your teeth carefully.

    b. Being bitten by a bull-ant is not fun.

9. Write ACTIVE or PASSIVE after the verb in these sentences.

    a. I was bitten _____ by a bull-ant.

    b. The bull-ant bit _____ me.

    c. The dog has eaten _____ my lunch.

    d. My lunch was eaten _____ by the dog.

10. Write COMPOUND or COMPLEX after each sentence.

    a. The dog came to the party and the cat came, too. _____

    b. You should visit Uluru because it is an interesting place. _____

    c. When you visit be sure to bring a camera. _____

| NONE WRONG ☐ | 1-2 WRONG ☐ | 3-4 WRONG ☐ | 5 OR MORE WRONG ☐ |
| (excellent) | (good) | (pass) | (more work needed) |

Text Type:

LITERARY DESCRIPTION

COHESION: SYNONYMS, ANTONYMS, COLLOCATION

Texts hold together in different ways. One is the use of word associations (chains) formed by **synonyms** (words of similar meaning) such as *chuckle* and *laugh*, or **antonyms**, words of opposite meaning such as *free* and *caught*. Another way is the use of **collocation**, a term used for words that are used together (co-locate, put together), as in all kinds of words used with a particular thing.

For instance, with *river* you might find, *bank, water, flood, gush, bottle, swirl, pool* ... and many others.

The River Bank

Never in his life had he seen a river before – this sleek, sinuous, full-bodied animal, chasing and chuckling, gripping things with a gurgle and leaving them with a laugh, to fling itself on fresh playmates that shook themselves free, and were caught and held again. All was a-shake and a-shiver – glints and gleams and sparkles, rustle and swirl, chatter and bubble. The Mole was bewitched, entranced, fascinated ...

and when tired at last, he sat on the bank, while the river chattered to him, a babbling procession of the best stories in the world, sent from the heart of the earth to be told at last to the insatiable sea.

The Wind in the Willows, Chapter 1
Kenneth Grahame

1. Read through the text and find synonyms for the following words. Write them in the spaces.

    a. fascinated _____   _____

    b. glints   _____   _____

    c. a-shake   _____

2. Write synonyms for the underlined words. Use a thesaurus if you wish.

    a. an <u>exciting</u> book _____

    b. a <u>beautiful</u> scene _____

c. a <u>very good</u> film _____

d. a <u>clever</u> writer _____

e. <u>throw</u> a ball_____

3. Write antonyms for these words.

laughing _____   good _____

leaving _____   clever _____

interesting _____   dark _____

quick _____   find _____

beautiful _____   fresh _____

4. The author describes the river as an animal. Write as many words and phrases as you can find in the passage that are used to describe this animal and what it does (that is, a collocation of words).

_____

_____

_____

5. Write a collocation of words (words that go together) to describe the sea, its surroundings and what it does.

Shore, wave … _____

_____

_____

_____

_____

MORE ACTION

• Write a literary description of your own to describe a river, the sea, the desert or whatever you would like to choose. (See Literary Description, p. 82.) You may wish to use a comparison, as Kenneth Grahame did, with an animal or bird.

• Write another brief literary description of a rainbow. Use the colour family of words: red, orange, yellow, green, blue, indigo and violet.

Text Type:

EXPLANATION

COHESION: REFERENCE TIES; WORD FAMILIES

Reference ties form links in writing. They help texts to hold together, to cohere. One type of link is the substitution of a pronoun or pronominal adjective for a noun, as in:

⌐ Plants grow in the soil.

└ They take nourishment from it.

These links are called reference ties because they refer to the noun they represent. Using these words not only creates links in the text but it stops us from repeating the noun again and again.

Other types of links in text are **word families** or **word sets**. They might be related in various ways, such as

"part" – "whole"

plant ⌐ root
        stem
        leaves

or by class or type as in

plant ⌐ vegetable
        tree
        shrub

How Plants Grow

1. Write in the missing links. Pick from the pronouns and pronominal adjectives in the box. You may use a word many times. The first one is done for you.

they	its	They	it	It
their	you	Their	them	which

Plants take nourishment from the soil in _____which_____ _____they_____ grow.

_____ take _____ through _____ roots. _____ take nourishment

through _____ leaves, also. _____ roots take moisture and mineral salts

from the soil and the leaves take carbon dioxide from the air. In the leaves there are tiny cells containing chlorophyll that gives the plant _____ green colour and

helps to turn the gas, water and salts into nourishment. The cells need light and

sunshine to do _____ work, so that the plants will grow tall. If _____ want

to study plants _____ will need to study botany. _____ is the science of plant life.

2. What pronouns or pronominal adjectives would you use instead of the words in
brackets. Write the new words in the spaces.

  a. Plants need sunlight. (Sunlight) _____ helps (plants) _____ grow.

  b. The roots take water and minerals from the soil. (The soil) _____

    must be kept moist, so the roots can do (the roots') _____ work properly.

  c. Chlorophyll gives the plants (the plants') _____ green colour.

3. Write the word families. Think of as many as you can.

	(Parts)		(Parts)
Plants	_____	Tree	_____
(whole)	_____	(whole)	_____
	_____		_____
	_____		_____

4. Write more members of these word families.

  a. shrub (parts) _____

  b. flowers (types) _____

  c. garden (parts) _____

  d. forest (parts) _____

  e. vegetable (types) _____

MORE ACTION

- In your own book, write your own explanation entitled *Why Plants Need Sunlight*.
(See Explanation, p. 85.) Circle the pronouns and pronominal adjectives.
- Write "qualities" for each of these words: *trees, flowers, rainforests, botanical
gardens,* e.g. vegetables: delicious, nourishing.

Text Type:

PROCEDURE

CONNECTIVES

Connectives are "signal words". Their main tasks are to join up sentences and tell us what is coming next or in what order things are done. For example, *First,* set the table. Connectives are different from conjunctions like *and, but* or *because* that join up parts of sentences. Both conjunctions and connectives help to hold texts together.

Preparing Breakfast

Ingredients
Cutlery: knives, forks, spoons
Table mats or table cloth
Plates and bowls
Mugs and glasses
Jug
Sugar, milk, cereal, bread, butter, jam, vegemite, juice
Toaster

Method
- *First, set table.*
- *Second, pour milk into jug.*
- *Next, pour juice into glasses.*
- *Now, tip cereal into bowls.*
- *Meanwhile, plug in the toaster.*
- *Finally, call everyone to breakfast!*

1. There are many examples of time connectives in this procedure. (See Procedure, p. 88.) Write them below.

   _____

   _____

2. Here are three connectives. Write a sentence for each one to describe how you set the table for breakfast.

   To begin _____

   _____

   After that _____

   _____

And finally _____

_____

3. Write the time connectives in the correct columns in the box.

At first   After a while   Then   Finally   To conclude
To start with   The next thing to do   At the commencement   In the end

BEGINNING	MIDDLE	END

You use connectives to make things clearer as in *for example,* to show results as in *therefore,* to add information as in *again* and to show conditions, as in *nevertheless.*

4. In your own book or folder, finish these sentences which begin with the following connectives. Use your own ideas.

In other words . . . ;   As a result . . . ;   Furthermore . . . ;   However . . . .

5. Finish this paragraph by filling in the spaces. The connectives are underlined.

I like to prepare breakfast. <u>In particular</u> _____

_____

<u>However</u> _____

_____

<u>Because of this</u> _____

_____

MORE ACTION

- Here are more connectives. *To be more precise, As a matter of fact, Because of this, Moreover, Despite this, On the contrary, In any case, Meanwhile.* In your own book folder, write sentences to follow each one.
- Write your own procedure for *Feeding the Dog* (or other pet), *Doing the Shopping at a Supermarket* or *Playing My favourite Game.* Before you start read about Procedures on p. 88.

Text Type:

FACTUAL DESCRIPTION

PARAGRAPHS

Paragraphs are parts of a larger piece of writing. They are "bundles" of information about a main idea and make texts easier to read and easier to write.

The length of a paragraph can vary from a simple sentence to a large number of sentences. Each paragraph nearly always contains a topic sentence that pinpoints the main idea. The **topic sentence** usually comes at the beginning of the paragraph.

Each new paragraph begins on a new line. It can be indented like this:

Next, there are the brass instruments

or separated from the last paragraph by a space like this:

. . . the trombone and the tuba.

Finally, there are the percussion instruments.

The Orchestra

The modern orchestra consists of a group of musicians who play various kinds of instruments. The players are led by a conductor, who directs them.

In the orchestra the instruments are grouped. There are the strings. They consist of the violin, viola, cello, double bass and harp.

Then there is the woodwind family. These are the flute, the piccolo, the oboe, the cor anglais, the clarinet and the bassoon.

Next, there are the brass instruments. They are the French horn, the trumpet, the trombone and the tuba.

Finally, there are the percussion instruments. These include the drums, cymbals, triangles and bells.

The orchestra, as we know it today, developed in the 17th century. It appeared in churches, theatres and the courts of Louis XIV and Charles II.

1. Write the topic sentences for each paragraph in the above factual description. (See Factual Description, p. 86.)

_____

_____

_____

_____

_____

_____

_____

2. Write three connectives that begin paragraphs.

_____ _____ _____

3. **a.** Divide this short factual description into paragraphs, using forward slashes like this /.

Ballet

The dancing skills needed to dance in a ballet are many. Every step and movement has to be learnt and carried out with precision. Other parts of the ballet are the story or libretto. Most ballets tell a story and part of the impact of the ballet comes through it. Then there is the choreography which is the sequence of steps and movements carried out by the dancers: a choreographer's task is very demanding. Next, there is the music. This is a very important part of the ballet and is often written specially for a ballet. Finally, we have the scenery and costumes. These set the scene and provide the necessary background for the ballet dancers.

b. Write the factual description, with paragraphs, in your own book or folder.

4. Finish these paragraphs.

A band consists of _____

_____ .

An important person is the lead singer. He/She _____

_____ .

Pop bands are very _____

_____ .

MORE ACTION

- Write a factual description of your favourite pop group or band. (See Factual Description, p. 86.) Say what you think makes the group special.
  Be sure to use suitable paragraphs.

Text Type:

FACTUAL RECOUNT

CORRECT USAGE

It is important to use correct grammar when we speak and write. Some common errors are using the wrong part of the verb as in *We seen him*, instead of the correct *We saw him*; using the wrong pronoun, as in *Him and me went*, instead of the correct *He and I went*; using double negatives, as in *I haven't done nothing*, instead of the correct *I haven't done anything;* and using slang in writing a serious letter, as in *I'm static!* instead of *I'm really excited!* Other common errors are using the wrong *homonym* (words that sound the same, but have different spellings) as in *grate, great.*

It is quite acceptable to use colloquial (everyday) expressions when you are talking to friends or writing a letter like the following, provided you do not overuse them *(I'm stoked!* or *Cool!).*

Letter to Mum

Dear Mum,

I'm (havin, having) a (grate, great) time (hear, here) with Dino. He's (gotta, got to) be (me, my) best friend, I'm (tellin, telling) (you, ya).

(Him and me, He and I) (saw, seen) (a, an) extra super movie last (night, knight) and we (done, did) some (fishin, fishing) in the afternoon. Didn't catch (nothing, anything) though.

Tomorrow, Dino's dad is taking Dino and (I, me) to the beach for the (hole, whole) weekend. I'm really stoked! (Your, You're) the greatest!!

Love,

Johnno

1. Cross out the wrong words in Johnno's letter to his Mum. Leave the correct words.

2. Write *did* or *done* in the spaces.

   a. We _____ our work.

   b. They have _____ a great job.

   c. We _____ our best.

   d. Dino and I have _____ all the shopping.

   e. They _____ very well.

3. Write *I* or *me* in the spaces.

a. Dino and ____ went to the movies.

b. Give the book to Mum or _____ .

c. They came with Bill and ____ .

d. My brother and ____ are twins.

e. Let's divide it between you and _____ .

4. Write *saw* or *seen* in the spaces.

a. I _____ him at the movies.

b. We have _____ lots of dolphins.

c. They _____ us at the zoo.

d. Have you _____ that show?

5. Write *sank* or *sunk; rang* or *rung; sang* or *sung* in the spaces.

a. The ship _____ last week.

b. The golfer _____ the putt.

c. We _____ the doorbell.

d. They have _____ the doorbell many times.

e. I _____ in the choir.

6. Do this correct grammar wiggleword.

ACROSS

1. I (saw, seen) the movie.

2. Give that to Jim and (I, me).

3. We have (saw, seen) the match.

4. The phone (rang, rung) loudly.

5. We have (did, done) our best.

DOWN

1. Have you (saw, seen) him?

2. Come with Maria and (I, me).

3. We (sang, sung) loudly.

4. I have (rang, rung) my brother.

5. He (did, done) it.

MORE ACTION

• Listen to the radio or watch television and make a list of the different examples of incorrect usage you hear. Collect examples over the week. You will be surprised how many you find!

Text Type:

EXPOSITION

MISUSED WORDS AND WORD ORIGINS

Many **words are misused** in speaking and writing. Sometimes, two words are confused, as in *insure* and *assure*; at other times they are used ungrammatically, as in *I rung yesterday*. (*Rang* is the correct past tense; *rung* is the past participle and must be used with an auxiliary verb, as in *I had rung yesterday*.)

A dictionary will give you the exact meaning of words, like *insure* and *assure*. Also, dictionaries will often give you the origin of the word, which helps to explain its meaning as in *emigrate* (from Latin: *e* – out of; *migrare* to move) and *immigrate* (from Latin, *im* – into; *migrare* to move).

TV is Good for Students

I will argue that TV is good for students. It helps to build (their, there) knowledge and I can't think of (anything, anythink) more entertaining.

Some believe that TV (effects, affects) students' studies, but this is not so, provided that they do not watch it (too, to) much.

Besides, students probably wouldn't do (nothing, anything) if they weren't watching TV. There are many valuable shows on TV I (insure, assure) you and TV is probably not much different (to, from) reading, anyway. Again, if you rely on books, you have to have a (loan, lend) of them and that is (real, really) time consuming.

I hope that you (except, accept) my argument that TV is good for students. I rest (my, me) case.

1. Read through this exposition and cross out the misused words. (See Exposition, p. 86.)

2. Cross out the misused words in these sentences.

   a. I hope we do not (loose, lose) the game because we (began, begun) so well.

   b. They (come, came) to tell us that they had just (emigrated, immigrated) to Australia.

   c. There are (fewer, less) cows in the (diary, dairy).

   d. The cow (laid, lay) down near where the hen (laid, lay) an egg.

e. Would you (loan, lend) me a dollar? I need a (loan, lend).

f. Divide these sweets (among, between) the four of you and see that nothing (is, are) wasted.

g. I could (of, have) (rang, rung) you last night.

3. In your own book or folder, write a sentence for each word in the pairs.
Use your dictionary to check the exact meanings.

employer	practice	export	precede
employee	practise	import	proceed
receipt	stationery	lightening	bought
recipe	stationary	lightning	brought

4. Cross out the wrong word and write the reason the word is incorrect.

a. I (seen, saw) the movie. _____

_____

b. The golfer (sank, sunk) the putt. _____

_____

c. (My, Me) brother is sick._____

_____

d. He and (me, I) went to school. _____

_____

e. I could (of, have) won. _____

_____

f. I (laid, lay) on the couch._____

_____

MORE ACTION
- Write an exposition arguing that TV is bad for you. (See Exposition, p. 86.)
- Use a good dictionary to find the origin of these words and their meanings:

apiarist	pyjamas
ballerina	graffiti
telephone	verandah
thermometer	antibiotic
premature	circumnavigate
hippopotamus	pterodactyl

Text Type:

POETRY

FIGURATIVE LANGUAGE: METAPHOR, PERSONIFICATION

Poetry is full of clever words used in clever ways. One example is **figures of speech**. These include interesting comparisons such as the **simile** in which things are compared, using *like* or *as*: *like a lion in battle* or *as good as gold*. Another is the **metaphor** in which things are compared directly, as in "*The moon was a ghostly galleon, tossed upon cloudy seas*" (Alfred Noyes). **Personification** is a special kind of metaphor in which the non-person thing compared is given human qualities, as in "*the morn, in russet mantle clad, walks o'er the dew of yon high eastern hill*" (Shakespeare). Sometimes a whole poem can rely on an **extended metaphor**, as in the poem below.

Wild Bulls at the Traffic Lights

The wild bulls stand
snorting,
pawing
the hard earth.
They strain to leap
roaring
at
the lonely matador,
but are stopped
by the red glare
of his eye. . .
Strange for bulls!

Gordon Winch

1. a. Who or what are the wild bulls?

_____

b. What points of comparison are there between the wild bulls in the poem and real wild bulls. _____

c. Why is the fact that these wild bulls have stopped at the traffic lights "Strange for bulls"?

_____

d. Finish this sentence.

In this extended metaphor, _____ are compared with_____.

2. In his poem, *The Beach*, William Hart-Smith uses this metaphor: *"The beach is a quarter of golden fruit, a soft ripe melon . . . "*

    a. Write some metaphors of your own to finish these sentences.

        The beach is _____ .

        The sea is _____ .

        The sky is _____ .

    b. In your own book or folder, write some metaphors in couplets, like these.

        Streams of cars in the traffic;   A bull in the paddock roaring;
          A line of ants on the path   An angry father calling.

    c. Here are some well-known metaphoric sayings. Write in your own book or folder what each one means.

       Having food for thought; Blowing your own trumpet; Getting into hot water; Leaving no stone unturned; Burning the candle at both ends; Letting the cat out of the bag; Skating on thin ice; Not having the ghost of a chance; Playing second fiddle; Splitting hairs.

3. In his famous poem, *The Daffodils,* William Wordsworth wrote this example of personification: *The waves beside them danced, but they outdid the sparkling waves in glee.*

Write your own examples of personification to complete the following sentences as in *The flowers stood in line.*

    a. The wind whispered _____ .

    b. The waves roared _____ .

    c. The sun smiled _____ .

    d. The trees spoke softly _____ .

    e. The creek sang _____ .

MORE ACTION

- Look through some collections of poetry in your library to find good examples of similes, metaphors and personification. Make a list of them. (See Poetry, p. 84).
- Write your own poem on a topic which interests you.

Text Type:

LITERARY RECOUNT: DRAMA

APOSTROPHE S: POSSESSION, CONTRACTION

The **apostrpohe** has two main uses: to show ownership with nouns and pronouns, as in *my sister's dog,* and to indicate where letters are left out, as in *I'm telling you.*

A good rule to help you place the apostrophe with ownership is: **When something is owned, place the apostrophe after the last letter of the owner.** This rule always works.

My Dad's Strong

CHARACTERS: Jimbo, Tilly, Mick, Charlie and Emma
SCENE: After school in Jimbo's backyard.

ACT I Scene 1
The children's voices are heard. They are talking in a spirited manner.

JIMBO: I'm telling you. My dad's strong. He can lift me and my sister's dog up.

TILLY: He's not as strong as my dad. My dad's really strong. He can lift me, my sister's dog and my sister up.

MICK: You'll have to agree that my dad's stronger. He can lift me, my two sisters' dogs – and my two sisters up.

CHARLIE: Not bad! But my dad's stronger. You'd better believe it! He can lift me, my two sisters' dogs, my two sisters – and Mum up.

EMMA: Tough, you guys, but my dad's stronger. He can lift me, my two sisters' dogs, my two sisters and Mum up – and give a victory wave with the other hand!

1. Read through *My Dad's Strong.*

   a. Draw a square around the words that contain an apostrophe of possession (ownership).

   b. Underline the words that contain an apostrophe of contraction (words left out).

2. Use the rule to place the apostrophe of ownership in these sentences.

a. All their dads arms must have been strong.

b. There were five childrens dads.

c. Emmas dad was really strong and so was Charlies.

d. There were many sisters dogs.

e. The mens arms must have been tired.

3. Place the apostrophes of contraction in the correct places.

a. I dont believe that theyve told the truth. Thats for sure!

b. Whats a tall tale if youre among friends!

c. Cmon dont try to tell me its true.

d. Hes very strong and shes strong too.

e. Wheres the truth in that? Its a pack of lies!

4. Place the apostrophes of possession and contraction in these sentences.

a. Im sure that Jimbos and the other childrens stories made them laugh, arent you?

b. Ive heard tall stories about sports persons records, havent you?

c. The mens tall stories and the womens tall stories didnt ring true, but were still laughing, arent you?

5. Place the apostrophes in the correct places. Watch out! Some do not need apostrophes.

a. the womens feet

b. the five actors stories

c. the ladies hats

d. Charlies mum

e. the girls school

f. Its a fine day.

g. I saw its head.

h. I dont think Ill be there.

i. Weve seen its two babies.

j. Ive come to see their play.

MORE ACTION

- In your own book, write a scene from a play like this one. Make up your own tall stories.
- Test out your friends on apostrophes of possession. If they put them in the wrong places, teach them the rule at the top of this unit.

Text Type:

NARRATIVE

PUNCTUATION IN DIRECT AND INDIRECT SPEECH

Direct speech is what is actually spoken. It is shown by speech marks (quotation marks) in writing, as in *"What's the Joke?" said Jo.* **Indirect speech** does not say what is actually spoken. It reports what is being or has been said, as in *Jo asked what was the joke*. No speech marks are needed. The **main stops** that we use in both forms are the **comma**, the **full stop**, the **question mark**, the **semicolon** and the **colon**. **Brackets** and **dashes** can be used, also.

The Go-Cart Kids

Andrew and Jason were sitting in the McIntyre's drive, with pieces of Andrew's go-cart motor all around them. They were laughing like mad.

"What's the joke?" said Jo with a friendly grin. She sat down beside them.

"Look what Jason did!" Andrew held up two parts of the motor and went off into new fits of laughter.

Jo smiled politely: she didn't get the joke.

"Well, that piece doesn't fit anywhere else," said Jason excitedly. "I swear it doesn't!"

Jenny Pausacker

1. a. Write the question that is in direct speech.

   _____

   b. Write the two exclamations that are in direct speech.

   _____

   _____

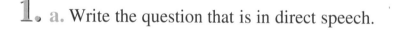

The **comma** is used to separate pauses in writing. Commas are used to separate nouns, adjectives and adverbs; after introductory words, and to separate long parts of a sentence. The full stop is used at the end of a statement or command.

2. a. Place capital letters, commas and full stops where you think they are needed in the following sentences:

the go-cart kids who lived in the suburbs were enthusiastic imaginative young and active children consequently they had lots of fun adventures and excitement

b. Find the three commas in the *The Go-Cart Kids*. Write why they are there in your own book or folder.

3. Punctuate the following examples of direct speech. Write in this text or rewrite in your own book or folder.

a. do you have a go-cart asked tony not me exclaimed andy i have a really fast manœuverable red billy-cart though

b. jos go-cart has stalled on the corner said ted oh no exclaimed jason what will she do

4. In your own book or folder, rewrite the passages from Exercise 3 in indirect speech. You will have to change some words and leave others out. Start off the first this way. Tony asked Andy if . . .

The **colon** is used to list more information, as in *Kids like to ride the following*: *trail bikes, go-carts, billy-carts, skateboards* and *razor scooters*.
The **semi-colon** is used to provide a stop between linked or balanced ideas, as in *I like go-carts; they're fun*. **Semi-colons** are also used to separate items in a long list, as in *two billy carts; five bikes; two razor scooters and their riders; roller blades and skates*.

5. Punctuate the following with colons or semi-colons.

a. I race every week its fun. **b.** Bring along these items a warm sweater, a helmet, goggles, glasses and an old pair of jeans. **c.** Jed has a new go-cart its magnificent!

d. The go-cart has a motor many other items like a brake excellent steering mechanism and beautiful ball-bearing wheels. **e.** I like go-carts Kim likes billy-carts.

MORE ACTION

- The **dash** is used to show sudden changes in thought or an unfinished sentence, as in *I can't see the – Oh, yes I can!* Another use is to enclose extra information. **Brackets** are used for the same purpose and come in pairs, as in *(I nearly forgot that)* . . .
- Write a story about a really exciting happening: a go-cart or billy-cart ride; a canoe ride down rapids; abseiling; a fast race on a trail bike; a ski trip; or horse-riding. Spice up your writing with colons, semi-colons, dashes and brackets.

TAKE A TEST 4

REVISION: UNITS 24 – 32

1. Finish these sentences by filling in the missing words.

a. Synonyms are words with _____ meanings.

b. Antonyms are words with _____ meanings.

c. For example, *fast* and *quick* are _____ .

d. *Good* and *bad* are _____ .

2. Write a synonym for each of these words:

a. beautiful _____   c. jump _____

b. fast _____   d. clever _____

3. Write an antonym for each of these words:

a. good _____   c. skinny _____

b. sunny _____   d. high _____

4. Write a collocation (words that go together) for the word "river". Start this way:

River: <u>bank, water</u> _____

_____

5. Write a word family for each of the following (at least five in each).

boat (parts) _____

_____

tree (parts) _____

_____

fruit (types) _____

_____

6. Finish these sentences.

a. Connectives are _____ words. Their main

task is to join sentences and tell us what is coming _____.

b. Write two more time connectives to continue this list.

To begin, _____ , _____

7. Correct the following sentences. Cross out the misued words. Write the correct words in the spaces.

a. (Him and me) _____ went to the football.

b. We (sung) _____ a few songs.

c. We didn't win but we (done) _____ our best.

d. (Me and her) _____ (seen) _____ the movie.

e. Jim went with Maria and (I) _____ .

8. Cross out the misused words.

a. They (come, came) to ask for a (lend, loan) of my racquet.

b. Split up this money (between, among) the five of you.

c. I could (of, have) (rang, rung) you last night.

9. Place apostrophes in the correct places.

a. my dads workshop

b. the childrens party

c. my two sisters friends.

10. Write these sentences in direct speech.

a. I said that I would see them at the beach.

_____

b. I told her that I was going home.

_____

| NONE WRONG (excellent) | ☐ | 1-2 WRONG (good) | ☐ | 3-4 WRONG (pass) | ☐ | 5 OR MORE WRONG (more work needed) | ☐ |

Appendix: Text Types

INTRODUCTION

When you refer to these text types you will be able to see how they are made up. This will help you with your writing and your understanding of grammar. The different types are in alphabetical order under Literary and Factual Texts.

LITERARY TEXT TYPES

LITERARY DESCRIPTION

What it is

A literary description describes, in a literary way, a particular thing such as a scene, an animal, a person or something that happens in nature. It can be part of a narrative or other literary text.

Its social purpose

Its purpose is to focus our attention on a particular thing and make us more aware of what it is really like through the detailed description.

How it is made up

In it you will find:
- An introduction to what is described
- A description of the features of the subject in a literary way: what a person or thing looks like, its qualities, the way it behaves and other features that make it special
- An evaluation of the subject during the description or at the end.

Grammar in a Literary Description

In a literary description you may find:
- Nouns, pronouns and noun groups: *rays, Edward; me; the two horsemen*
- Adjectives: *chilly, rocky*
- Relating (linking) and action verbs: *were, have; hid, ride*
- Adverbs and adverbials: *again; from the heart, with a gurgle*
- Figurative language such as similes and metaphors: *like an intruder; a river – this sleek, sinuous, full-bodied animal.*

LITERARY RECOUNT

What it is

A literary recount, like a factual recount, retells something that happened. It is called a literary recount because it is written in a creative, entertaining way. A literary recount can also be part of a narrative.

Its social purpose

Its purpose is to entertain by recounting a series of events. It can also express feelings.

How it is made up

In it you will find:

- An orientation that sets the scene and tells us who is in the story and when and where it is happening
- A record of events, usually in the order they occurred
- A reorientation that rounds off the events. It ends the recount
- Sometimes a literary recount finishes with the author's personal feelings about the events. This is called a coda.

Grammar in a Literary Recount

In a literary recount you may find:

- Common and proper nouns that identify people and things: *ice, Shackleton*
- Personal pronouns: *he, you*
- Action verbs in the past tense: *crushed, made*
- Relating (linking) verbs: *is, are*
- Adverbial phrases: *in Antarctica*
- Connectives indicating time: *now, next*

NARRATIVE

What it is

A narrative tells a story. It entertains and makes the reader think and feel about the happenings and characters in it. A narrative often presents a problem for the characters and may contain unexpected happenings and surprise endings.

Its social purpose

Its purpose is to entertain us and teach us new things about people and the world.

How it is made up

In it you will find:

- An orientation, that sets the scene in time and place and tells us who is in the story. It alerts the reader to what will follow.
- A complication. It contains the events that raise complications and problems in the lives of the characters.
- A resolution, in which the problems are usually worked out.
- The coda, which is the last part of the narrative, that often shows how the character or characters have been changed. It rounds off the narrative.

Grammar in a Narrative

In a narrative you may find:

- Common and proper nouns: *water, Ka Li*
- Action verbs in the past tense: *fixed, yelled*
- Direct speech (dialogue): *"Grab my hand," he yelled.*
- Adjectives to build noun groups: *yellow water*
- Time connectives and conjunctions to show sequence of events: *now, then; and, as*
- Adverbs and adverbial phrases: *relentlessly; towards him.*

POETRY

What it is
- Poetry is a special form of speaking or writing. It was called "The best words in the best order" by Samuel Taylor Coleridge, the famous poet.
- Poetry can fit into many other types of text: it can tell a story in a ballad (a narrative poem); it can be a literary description or a recount and more.
- The most important point about poetry is that it can do so many things: it can be lots of fun; it can be very sad; it can make us think deeply. Above all, it is very enjoyable.

Its social purpose
- Poetry achieves a range of social purposes. These include expressing feelings, thinking about experiences, telling a story, describing things and using striking language.

How it is made up
- Many types of poems and each one is different: a ballad or narrative poem is usually long; a limerick is short; a sonnet has 14 lines. Each type of poem has its own shape and make up.
- Some forms of poetry are the ballad, lyric, limerick, haiku and concrete poem (that has a shape like the thing it describes).

Grammar in Poetry
- Because there are so many forms of poetry, there are many different examples of grammar. In fact, you may find all the grammar described in this book in poetry.
- Special features of poetry are rhyme, rhythm and figurative (colourful and creative) language.
- Because poetry is best if it is read aloud, sound effects, like rhyme, rhythm and repetition, are very important.

REVIEW

What it is
A review is a response to a text. In it a writer or speaker tells briefly what the text is about and says what he or she thinks of it. That is, the reviewer gives a description of the characters, a summary of the story and an evaluation of the writing.

Its social purpose
Its purpose is to decide on the value and appeal of the text. That is, whether it has value and whether you like it.

How it is made up
In it you will find:
- A text description might contain information about the author, the setting and a description of the main characters in the story.
- A summary of the incidents (what happens).
- What the reviewer thinks of the text. (Did I enjoy it? Is it well written and why? Would I ask someone else to read, view or hear it?)

Grammar in a Review

In a review you may find:

- Relating (linking) verbs in the present tense: *is, have*
- Action verbs in the past tense: *caught*
- Noun groups: *the class newspaper*
- Articles: *the, a*
- Long (complex) sentences: *Melanie's main victim is …who is supported…*
- Evaluative language: *really exciting novel*
- Adverbial phrases and clauses: *in the class newspaper; as it tells a story.*

FACTUAL TEXT TYPES

DISCUSSION

What it is

A discussion presents arguments or points of view for both sides of an issue or topic.

Its social purpose

- Its purpose is to allow us to consider different views before we make up our minds about an issue.

How it is made up

In it you will find:

- A statement that outlines an issue or topic
- Background information on the topic
- The arguments for
- The arguments against
- A summary and a final discussion or recommendation.

Grammar in a Discussion

In a discussion you may find:

- Nouns and noun groups: *people, sport; a friendly, social game*
- Relating (linking) and thinking verbs; present tense: *is; think, seems*
- Conjunctions and connectives: *and, because; also, again*
- Adverbs; modal adverbs: *carefully; certainly*
- Clauses linked by conjunctions; compound sentences: *… more railways because …, more roads and more railways*
- Evaluative language: *vital importance.*

EXPLANATION

What it is

- An explanation tells how something works or why it occurs the way it does.

Its social purpose

- Its purpose is to help us understand how things work and why they are like they are in our world.

How it is made up

In it you will find:

- An introduction that states what is to be explained
- The how or why explanation in a series of steps in order
- A final summing up statement
- It may include diagrams, illustrations and charts or tables.

Grammar in an Explanation

In an explanation you may find:

- Action verbs: *acclimatised, sunrise*
- Conjunctions: *and, because*
- Nouns and noun groups; abstract nouns: *bushfires, hardy Australian plants; chance*
- Adjectives: *definite, imported*
- Adverbs and adverbial phrases: *well, from the soil*
- Complex sentences; technical language: *In the leaves there are tiny cells containing chlorophyll that gives the plant...*

EXPOSITION

What it is

An exposition argues a case for or against a point of view or belief.

Its social purpose

Its purpose is to argue a case, to persuade a person or persons to agree with the argument and to act as a result.

How it is made up

In it you will find:

- An opening statement that describes the position taken
- Stages in the argument that make the case
- A concluding statement to reinforce the point of view or belief.

Grammar in an Exposition

In an exposition you may find:

- Nouns, common and abstract: *people; happiness*
- Pronouns: *it, they*
- Verbs, action, relating (linking): *living, is*
- Modals: adverbs and verbs: *certainly, probably; may*
- Conjunctions and connectives: *and, but; again, besides*
- Compound and complex sentences: *Some people believe that TV affects students' studies, but this is not so; some people can experience happiness, while others would be in despair.*
- Word families: *happiness, joy; misery, despair*
- Theme of clause: *Happiness*
- Rheme of clause: *is a state of mind.*

FACTUAL DESCRIPTION

What it is

A factual description describes, in a factual way, the features of a particular thing that is living or not, such as a particular dog or a particular mountain. (An information report usually describes a whole class of things.)

Its social purpose

Its purpose is to tell us more about particular things in our environment.

How it is made up
In it you will find:
- An introduction to what is being described
- A description of the physical and other qualities of the subject
- A comment about the worth of the subject.

Grammar in a Factual Description
In a factual description you may find:
- Nouns, pronouns and noun groups: *beagle, Ben; he, I; particles of brown, black and white*
- Adjectives which describe or classify: *gentle, affectionate; scent* hound
- Relating, thinking, feeling and action verbs: *is; believe; likes; take*
- Adverbs and adverbials: *up; above the desert.*

FACTUAL RECOUNT

What it is
A factual recount 'tells what happened'. It records a series of events in the order they occurred and states their importance.

Its social purpose
Its purpose is to present a record of a happening and to consider its value.

How it is made up
In it you will find:
- An orientation which gives you information about whom (the people or things involved), where (where it happened) and when (when it happened)
- A list of the things that happened in the order that they occurred
- Personal comments and other remarks in different parts of the text
- A "rounding off" (reorientation) that sums up the event and often concludes with what might happen in the future.

Grammar in a Factual Recount
In a factual recount you may find:
- Nouns and pronouns that identify people and things: *gulls; we*
- Action verbs in the past tense to refer to events: *went, saw*
- Conjunctions and connectives to show the sequence of events: *and; again, afterwards*
- Adverbs and adverbial phrases to show place and time: *overhead; in the sea, after a while*
- Adjectives to describe nouns: *tiny, silly*
- Apostrophes to show ownership and contraction: *the whale's tail; I'd like to go again*
- Paragraphs to indicate parts of text: *Last Sunday / Then we went.*

INFORMATION REPORT

What it is
An information report gives factual information about something. It mainly describes an entire class of things such as *planets, countries* or *mammals*. (A factual description usually describes a particular thing such as a *particular* bird with a *particular* name.)

Its social purpose

Its purpose is to give us information about a topic, usually a whole class of things.

How it is made up

In it you will find:

- A general statement about the subject
- Details of information such as physical characteristics and behaviour.
- Sometimes, a comment on the worth of the subject.

Grammar in an Information Report

- Nouns and pronouns: *giants, Great White Sharks; they*
- Action verbs, relating (linking) verbs: *eat, are, have*
- Present tense (timeless present): They *are* fearsome predators
- Phrases: *in temperate zones*
- Clauses SVO (Subject Verb Object): *juveniles eat squid*
- Paragraphs with topic sentences: *These mighty creatures...Mammals are animals whose babies...*

PROCEDURE

What it is

A procedure tells people how to do or make something. Recipes, rules of games, how to grow things and how to get from place to place are all procedures.

Its social purpose

A procedure tells people how to do or make things.

How it is made up

In it you will find:

- A goal, such as *How to Make Yuk Soup* or *How to Grow Tomatoes; How to get from A to B*
- A list of materials you will need
- The steps or instructions that show you what to do.

Grammar in a Procedure

In a procedure you may find:

- Commands: *Blow gently on...*
- Action verbs: *Remove, eat, wash*
- Common nouns: *pie, bag, gravy*
- Adjectives: *hot, small*
- Prepositions in adjectival and adverbial phrases: *of whales, with a long handle; near the shore*
- Connectives to show the sequence of steps: *Then, finally.*

Outcomes and Indicators

Key Outcomes Relating to Grammar

Although all English syllabus outcomes relate directly and indirectly to grammar, the following Talking and Listening, Reading and Writing outcomes provide the most tangible links with specific indicators in grammar understanding and learning.

New South Wales outcomes are used in this series – Teachers in other States should refer to specific State outcomes.

OUTCOMES CHECKLIST	Yes	Partly	No

Talking and Listening Outcomes

TS3.1 Communicates effectively for a range of purposes and with a variety of audiences to express well developed, well organised ideas dealing with more challenging topics	☐	☐	☐
TS3.2 Interacts productively and with autonomy in pairs and groups of various sizes and composition, uses effective oral presentation skills and strategies and listens attentively.	☐	☐	☐
TS3.3 Discusses ways in which spoken language differs from written language and how spoken language varies according to different contexts.	☐	☐	☐
TS3.4 Evaluates the organisational patterns of some more challenging spoken texts and some characteristic language features.	☐	☐	☐

Reading Outcomes

RS3.5 Reads independently an extensive range of texts with increasing content demands and responds to themes and issues.	☐	☐	☐
RS3.6 Uses a comprehensive range of skills and strategies appropriate to the type of text being read.	☐	☐	☐
RS3.7 Critically analyses techniques used by writers to create certain effects, to use language creatively, to position the reader in various ways and to construct different interpretations of experience.	☐	☐	☐
RS3.8 Identifies the text structure of a wider range of more complex text types and discusses how the charactcristic grammatical features work to influence readers' and viewers' understanding of texts.	☐	☐	☐

Writing Outcomes

WS3.9   Produces a wide range of well-structured and well-presented literary and factual texts for a wide variety of purposes and audiences using increasingly challenging topics, ideas, issues and written language features. ☐ ☐ ☐

WS3.10   Uses knowledge of sentence structure, grammar and punctuation to edit own writing. ☐ ☐ ☐

WS3.13   Critically analyses own texts in terms of how well they have been written, how effectively they present the subject matter and how they influence the reader. ☐ ☐ ☐

WS3.14   Critically evaluates how own texts have been structured to achieve their purpose and discusses ways of using related grammatical features and conventions of written language to shape readers' and viewers' understanding of texts. ☐ ☐ ☐

INDICTORS CHECKLIST

	Yes	Partly	No
1. Identifies and uses common, proper and collective nouns. (Unit 1)	☐	☐	☐
2. Identifies and uses abstract nouns. (Unit 2)	☐	☐	☐
3. Understands and uses number and gender with nouns. (Unit 3)	☐	☐	☐
4. Identifies and uses adjectives: descriptive, numeral, possessive. (Unit 4)	☐	☐	☐
5. Identifies and uses classifying and modal adjectives. (Unit 5)	☐	☐	☐
6. Identifies and uses demonstrative adjectives. (Unit 6)	☐	☐	☐
7. Understands and uses degree with adjectives. (Unit 6)	☐	☐	☐
8. Understands and the articles a, an and the. (Unit 7)	☐	☐	☐
9. Identifies and uses personal and possessive pronouns. (Unit 8)	☐	☐	☐
10. Identifies and uses relative, interrogative and demonstrative pronouns. (Unit 9)	☐	☐	☐
11. Understand and uses person, number and gender in pronouns. (Unit 10)	☐	☐	☐
12. Understands and uses nominative, objective and possessive case with pronouns. (Unit 11)	☐	☐	☐
13. Recognises and uses action, saying, thinking and relating verbs. (Unit 12)	☐	☐	☐
14. Understands and uses present, past and future tense with verbs, including timeless present. (Unit 13)	☐	☐	☐
15. Understands and uses active and passive voice with verbs. (Unit 13)	☐	☐	☐
16. Identifies and uses adverbs of manner, time and place. (Unit 14)	☐	☐	☐
17. Recognises and uses interrogative, modal and negative adverbs. (Unit 14)	☐	☐	☐
18. Identifies and uses prepositions. (Unit 15)	☐	☐	☐
19. Identifies and uses co-ordinate and subordinate conjunctions. (Unit 16)	☐	☐	☐
20. Recognises and uses noun (nominal/phrase) groups. (Unit 17)	☐	☐	☐
21. Recognises and uses verb groups, main and auxiliary verbs. (Unit 18)	☐	☐	☐

	Yes	Partly	No

22. Identifies and uses adjectival and adverbial prepositional phrases. (Unit 19) ☐ ☐ ☐

23. Identifies and uses sentences: statement, question, exclamation, command. (Unit 20) ☐ ☐ ☐

24. Identifies and uses principal and subordinate clauses. (Unit 21) ☐ ☐ ☐

25. Recognises and uses direct and indirect objects in clauses. (Unit 22) ☐ ☐ ☐

26. Identifies and uses theme and rheme in clauses. (Unit 22) ☐ ☐ ☐

27. Recognises compound and complex sentences. (Unit 23) ☐ ☐ ☐

28. Identifies and uses synonyms and antonyms. (Unit 24) ☐ ☐ ☐

29. Identifies and uses the cohesive devices of collocation. (Unit 24) ☐ ☐ ☐

30. Identifies and uses the cohesive devices of reference ties and word set (families). (Unit 25) ☐ ☐ ☐

31. Recognises and uses connectives. (Unit 26) ☐ ☐ ☐

32. Understand and uses paragraphs and topic sentences. (Unit 27) ☐ ☐ ☐

33. Understands and uses correct grammar in past tense/past participle, case, double negatives. (Unit 28) ☐ ☐ ☐

34. Understands and uses correct homonyms and apt use of colloquialisms. (Unit 28) ☐ ☐ ☐

35. Recognises and avoids misuse of words. (Unit 29) ☐ ☐ ☐

36. Understands and uses figurative language: simile, metaphor, personification. (Unit 30) ☐ ☐ ☐

37. Understands and uses correct punctuation: the apostrophe of possession and contraction. (Unit 31) ☐ ☐ ☐

38. Understands and uses direct and indirect speech. (Unit 32) ☐ ☐ ☐

39. Understands and uses the main punctuation marks: comma, full stop, question mark, semi-colon, colon, bracket, dash. (Unit 32) ☐ ☐ ☐

40. Identifies and understands the terms literary and factual text types (see text type appendix). ☐ ☐ ☐

41. Identifies and uses Literary Description (see text type appendix). ☐ ☐ ☐

42. Identifies and uses Literary Recount (see text type appendix). ☐ ☐ ☐

43. Identifies and uses Narrative (see text type appendix). ☐ ☐ ☐

44. Identifies and uses Poetry (see text type appendix). ☐ ☐ ☐

45. Identifies and uses Review (see text type appendix). ☐ ☐ ☐

46. Identifies and uses Discussion (see text type appendix). ☐ ☐ ☐

47. Identifies and uses Explanation (see text type appendix). ☐ ☐ ☐

48. Identifies and uses Exposition (see text type appendix). ☐ ☐ ☐

49. Identifies and uses Factual Description (see text type appendix). ☐ ☐ ☐

50. Identifies and uses Factual Recount (see text type appendix). ☐ ☐ ☐

51. Identifies and uses Information Report (see text type appendix). ☐ ☐ ☐

52. Identifies and uses Procedure (see text type appendix). ☐ ☐ ☐

Answers

UNIT 1

1. common nouns: whales, shore, gulls, fish, sea, boats, sheep. proper nouns: Sunday, Joanne, Danny Correto, White Horse Beach. collective nouns: pod, flock, school, convoy. **2.** sea, horse, cat, fish, whale, bone, star, sea, weed, pond, head, land, sand, bag, shore, line, boat, house. **3.** crowd of people; bunch of grapes; swarm of bees; string of pearls; stable of horses; troupe of actors; herd of elephants; batch of scones; squadron of planes; team of athletes. **4.** Captain Bagshaw, groups of people, gaggle of geese, herd of cattle, swarm of insects. **5.** student's answers.

UNIT 2

1. Happiness, State, Mind, happiness, despair, joy, misery, excitement, fear, distress, Happiness, feelings, state, mind. **2.** a. unhappiness. b. hopelessness. c. cruelty. d. ugliness. e. hate. f. boredom. **3.** a. joy, exhilaration, excitement, happiness, exuberance. b. grief, despair, misery, hopelessness, sadness. **4.** joy, happiness; doubt, uncertainty; sadness, misery; hate, loathing; bravery, courage; love, affection. **5.** pain, loneliness, pity, beauty, courage, sadness, health, sorrow, anger, greed.

UNIT 3

1. plural nouns: Mammals, animals, babies, cows, bulls, mammals, mammals, mammals, qualities, eggs, reptiles, babies. singular nouns: milk, mother, cow, calf, milk, earth, platypus, echidna, wombat, kangaroo, platypus, mammal, milk, body. **2.** mother F, milk N, cows F, mammals C, platypus C, animals C, kangaroo C, bulls M, babies C, earth N. **3.** a. babies, mothers. b. Kangaroos, mammals. c. qualities. d. Sheep, horses. **4.** tomatoes, berries, potatoes, grasses, leaves, larvae, fish (fishes very rarely), mangoes (mangos). **5.** sheep, geese, echidnas, wolves, oxen, mice, butterflies, turkeys, monkeys, flies. **6.** mare, duck, hen, sow, lioness, ewe, goose, cow, doe, bitch.

UNIT 4

1. a. sharp, chilly, dark, steady, rocky, bare, inhospitable, riding, particular, broad-brimmed, oilskin, spurred, identical, lonely, cloned, desolate, wintry, steaming. b. Two, first, two. c. their, Their, their, Their. **2.** student's answers. **3.** possible answers: b. large, white. c. thin (slim, tiny small), energetic (active). d. empty, light. e. careful thoughtful. **4.** a. two eyes, one small nose, twenty nails, ten toes. b. (i) my, your. (ii) their, (others will fit). (iii) my, (others will fit). her (others will fit. (iv) its. **5.** fearless explorer, beautiful flower, crowded bus, slithery snake, enormous elephant, exciting adventure, clever student, dense forest.

UNIT 5

1. classifying adjectives: native, Australian, gum, Eucalyptus, imported. modal adjectives: possible, certain, definite, slight. **2.** classifying adjectives: plastic, African, library, tiger, passenger, cotton, English, Japanese, Australian, daily. **3.** a. certain (definite, necessary). b. sure (certain). c. likely. d. definite, certain. **4.** certain, possible, probable, necessary, determined. **5.** student's answers. Some suggestions: Australian or native, school, slight, unlikely.

UNIT 6

1. a. those, That. b. great, greater, greatest; good, better, best; fast, faster, fastest; tough, tougher, toughest; small, smaller, smallest. **2.** a. That. b. Those. c. these or those. d. this or that. e. those. **3.** more wonderful, most wonderful. more agile, most agile. more competitive, most competitive. more spectacular, most spectacular. **4.** many, more, most; bad, worse, worst. little, less, least. good, better, best. **5.** brightest, best.

UNIT 7

1. 5 'the', 4 'a', 2 'an'. **2.** a. The (D), a (I). b. a (I), an (I). c. a (I), a (I). **3.** an argument, an eerie sound, a brave rabbit, an hour before dark, a wonderful novel, an heir to the throne, an itchy spot, an awful battle, an honourable act, an umbrella. **4.** a. The, the or an, The, the, an, a. b. an, a, an, a, a. **5.** The, A, The, The, A, The, The, The.

TAKE A TEST 1. REVISION: UNITS 1 – 7

1. a. name. b. proper. c. collection, group. **2.** common: zoo, elephants, gulls, whales, ocean. proper: Dubbo, Jan, Maria. collective: herd, flock, pod. **3.** abstract. **4.** a. happiness. b. abstract. **5.** a. P. b. P. c. S. d. P. e. S. f. S or P. **6.** berries, monkeys, sheep, leaves, flies, geese. **7.** a. mare. b. ewe. c. sow. d. goose. e. lioness. f. doe. **8.** descriptive: big, kind. numeral: three, two. possessive: my, their. **9.** a. classifying: Australian, library. modal: slight, certain. b. T. **10.** good, better, best; fast, faster, fastest; many, more, most. **11.** a. T. b. T.

UNIT 8

1. personal pronouns: He, he, I, him, he, I, him, He, I, He, it, I, I, it, you. b. possessive pronouns: mine, his. **2.** a. we, them b. I, He. c. I, him, he, me. d. You, They. **3.** possessive pronouns: mine, ours, yours, hers, theirs, its. **4.** a. He. b. They. c. She. d. They. e. he, She. **5.** correct personal pronouns: a. She. b. me. c. I. d. me. e. you.

UNIT 9

1. relative pronouns: who play, that everyone, which have, who can; Interrogative pronouns: who wants, what could, who could; Demonstrative pronouns: That is, This is, These are. **2.** a. who. b. that. c. which. d. whom. e. who. f. whom. **3.** a. Who. b. Whose. c. Which, (Whom, Whose, What). d. What. (Which). e. whom. **4.** a. That (This). b. These, (Those). c. Those. d. This, (That). e. These, (Those).

UNIT 10

1. b. I: 1st person, singular, masculine. he: 3rd person, singular, masculine. she: 3rd person, singular, feminine. her: 3rd person, singular, feminine. him: 3rd person, singular, masculine. it: 3rd person, singular, neuter. **2.** a. (i) they, them. (ii) I, me. (iii) he, she, it, him, her, it. (iv) you, you. b. she, her. **3.** a. (i) He, She. (ii) I, them. (iii) you. b. (i) 3rd person, singular, masculine; 3rd person, singular, feminine. (ii) 1st person, singular, masculine or feminine; 3rd person, plural, common. (iii) 2nd person, singular or plural, common or masculine and/or feminine.

UNIT 11

1. (clench on) his, His (to) hers, hers (to) his. **2.** a. (i) mine. (ii) them. (iii) he, she, it. b. (i) yours. (ii) her. (iii) them. (iv) They. (v) his. b. student's answers. c. student's answers.

UNIT 12

1. a. dart, dash, jig, jump, scamper, skate, scramble, strut, stride, slip, slide, amble, leap, lurch, crawl, creep, rove, romp, ramble, turn, trip, skid, skip, gambol. **2.** student's answers. **3.** possible answers a. consider, contemplate. b. Think. c. debated. d. believe. e. considered, debated. **4.** a. been. b. were. c. am, are, are. d. are. e. was, is. **5.** he is, you are, you have, there is, we are, she is, I have, they are, I am, they have.

UNIT 13

1. a. are, will grow, will weigh, are, have, are, eat, prefer, will eat, are found, were hunted, have decreased, are protected, have followed. b. possible answers: are, have, eat, prefer, are found, are protected. **2.** a. present. b. future. c. past. d. past. e. past. f. future. g. present. h. past. i. present. j. past. **3.** Great White Sharks are fierce and dangerous creatures. If you swim near them they eat you. They think you are a seal. They kill for food, not for pleasure. b. Great White Sharks will be fierce and dangerous creatures. If you will swim near them they will eat you. They will think you are a seal. They will kill for food, not for pleasure. **4.** a. Seals are eaten by the Great White Shark. b. Humans will be eaten by them, too. c. These sharks are protected by us in our waters. d. Many Great White Sharks were caught by men. e. A Great White Shark has been seen by me.

UNIT 14

1. Carefully, firmly, over, Then, cautiously, gently, very, immediately, too, quickly, inside, up, down, Frequently, near, Finally, quickly, Now, thoroughly. **2.** manner: carefully, firmly, cautiously, gently, very, too, quickly, thoroughly. time: Then, immediately, Frequently, Finally, Now. place: over, inside, up, down, near. **3.** student's answers. **4.** slowly, up, outside, under, carelessly, firstly, roughly, seldom or infrequently, nowhere. **5.** hungrily, carefully, cautiously, seriously, occasionally, greedily, thoroughly, immediately, completely, politely.

UNIT 15

1. a. in, of, at, for, for, in, in, for, at, in, underneath, to, through, to. b.+ c. in Bexley, of Sydney, at war, for toys, for food. in car, in Australia, for effort, at baths, in Botany Bay, underneath pier, to Brighton-le-Sands, through stormwater, to Bay. **2.** a. between. b. among. c. into. d. in. e. beside. f. besides. **3.** a. down, adverb. b. down, preposition. c. along, preposition. d. along, adverb. e. past, adverb. f. past, adjective.

UNIT 16

1. circle and, but. b. <u>Dad</u> and <u>I</u>, <u>event</u> and <u>I</u>, <u>netball'</u> but I really like <u>golf</u>, <u>arrived</u> and <u>caught</u>, <u>sandwiches</u> and <u>drinks</u>, <u>Dad</u> and <u>I</u>, <u>stand</u> and <u>watch</u>, <u>long</u> and <u>difficult</u>, <u>I</u> thought but <u>the players</u>, <u>far</u> and <u>straight</u>, <u>played well</u> but <u>did not win</u>, <u>great players</u> and <u>interesting people</u>. c. when we arrived, because it was a very warm day, after everyone had hit off, as they can hit the ball so far and so straight, although the result was close.
2. a. but. b. and. c. but. d. and. e. but. **3.** a. because. b. after. c. if, when. d. When. **4.** student's answers.

TAKE A TEST 2. REVISION: UNITS 8 – 16

1. a. instead of a noun. b. possessive. **2.** personal: It, He, They, We, you. possessive: mine, ours, theirs, ours, yours. **3.** relative: who, whom. interrogative: What, Whom, Whose. demonstrative: That, This, Those.
4. she: 3rd, singular, feminine. him: 3rd, singular, masculine. it: 3rd, singular, neuter. we: 1st, plural, common. **5.**
a. personal. b. possessive. c. possessive. d. personal. **6.** a. I, nominative. her, objective. she, nominative. them, objective. b. theirs, possessive. ours, possessive. **7.** a. action. b. thinking. c. caring. d. relating.
8. a. present. b. future. c. past. d. past. **9.** a. active. b. passive. **10.** slowly: manner. down: place. early: time. **11.**
into: preposition. across: preposition. past: adverb. **12.** co-ordinate: and, but. subordinate: because, when.

UNIT 17

1. a. Takers by Aidan. b. two equally nasty. c. victim in this. d. exposure in the class. e. exciting. **2.** a. This novel about bullies, an exciting piece of writing. b. She, a cruel and unfeeling person. c. Angus Burns, a true friend in every way. d. Lucy's parents, kind and understanding people e. The class newspaper, this unpleasant school bully. **3.** a. a, a school, an unfeeling school. b. a, a clever, a clever, well thought-out. **4.** student's answers. **5.** a. A well-written exciting novel for older students, an interesting and well-developed plot. b. The characters in an interesting novel for older students, well-drawn realistic and recognisable people.

UNIT 18

1. a. been. b. must. c. be. d. have, be undertaken. e. never be. **2.** had been crushed, knew, was, must sail, must be done, lashed, battered, would have to be undertaken, would be, would be, made, would perish, stranded, would never be rescued or would be rescued. **3.** a. were. b. was. c. will. d. have, had. e. will. **4.** Present tense: He is sailing, They are sailing. He is doing. They are doing. Past tense: He had sailed. They had sailed. He had done. They had done. **5.** a. sailed. b. crushed. c. lashed.

UNIT 19

1. Prepositions: in, of, from, of, on, with, in, of, in, into, from, in, with, around, with, with. Phrases + **2.** in a pot (adj.), of fertiliser (adj.), from a shop (adj.), of horse or cow manure (adj.), on the ground (adv.), with a long handle (adj.), in the ground (adv.), of fertiliser (adj.), in the hole (adv.). into the hole (adv.), from the pot (adv.) in the hole (adv.), with soil (adv.) around the tree (adv.), with mulch (adv.), with the hose (adv.).
3. a. adverbial. b. adverbial. c. adverbial. d. adjectival. e. adjectival. f. adjectival. g. adjectival. h. adverbial. i. adverbial. j. adjectival. **4.** adverbial phrase: underneath a tree, verb: are spread. **5.** adjectival. a. in the meadow. b. on a tree. c. in the pasture. d. of trees. e. beside the river. Each phrase describes or adds meaning to a noun.

UNIT 20

1. a. 11. b. Don't you agree? This must be better! **2.** a. Roads provide for flexible use because they need rail tracks. b. You can use a bicycle, bus, car or truck (if, when) you travel on a road. c. Roads are built in the country in order to open up the country areas. d. Roads are easier to use because you don't have to wait on stations and you don't have to 'follow' timetables. (Other answers are acceptable.) **3.** student's answers. **4.** a. full stop. b. ! c. ? d. ? e. full stop.

UNIT 21

1. we, They, one train, they, which, we, our population, A suitable mix. **2.** a. principal. b. subordinate. c. principal. d. subordinate. e. subordinate. f. principal. **3.** Trains are needed because they cause less pollution. Other people argue that we need more railways. Don't cut down the trees that help reduce erosion. We saw the men who were building the railway. We will need more railways when our population grows. **4.** Correct words: a. are. b. have. c. are. d. believe. e. are. **5.** a. adverbial clause. b. noun clause. c. adjectival clause.

UNIT 22

1. a. story. b. Kylie, the Kangaroo. c. it. d. the book. e. all the other kangaroos in Australia. **2.** a. Emily. b. me. c. me. d. her. e. her. **3.** Theme: a. It. b. Being bitten by a bull-ant. c. Again and again. d. Emily. e. That story. Rheme: a. was called Kylie the Kangaroo. b. would make anyone hop. c. I would read it. d. loved that story. e. was loved by Emily. **4.** a. The book was read to Emily by me. b. Kylie was bitten by the bull-ants. c. Other kangaroos were taught to hop by her. d. That story was loved by Emily. e. The story was liked by me, too.

UNIT 23

1. student's answers. **2.** You are permitted to climb Uluru but the Anangu do not like you to do it. Uluru is deep red and it appears to change colour at different times of the day. Uluru is sacred to the aboriginal people and they are the traditional owners. The Rock is 348 metres high and it is 9.4 kilometres around the base. **3.** that was compressed (adjectival). who arrived there (adjectival). which measures (adjectival). **4.** adverbial, adverbial clause of time, adverbial clause of reason. **5.** student's answers.

TAKE A TEST 3. REVISION: UNITS 17 – 23

1. The novel by Aidan Chambers, an interesting book, The characters in the novel, a good story. **2.** a. have been reading. b. had told, were reading. c. will have seen. **3.** a. in the library, adverbial. about trees, adjectival. b. of fertiliser, adjectival. c. to the shops, adverbial. in a pot, adjectival. **4.** a. statement. b. command. c. question. d. exclamation. **5.** a. subordinate. b. principal. c. principal. d. principal. e. subordinate. **6.** a. adverbial clause. b. noun clause. c. adjectival clause. **7.** direct: a. present. b. ball. c. book. d. story. indirect: a. me. b. them. c. me. d. James. **8.** a. Kylie b. Being bitten by a bull-ant. c. Always. **9.** a. passive. b. active. c. active. d. passive. **10.** a. compound. b. complex. c. complex.

UNIT 24

1. a. bewitched, entranced. b. gleams, sparkles. c. a-shiver. **2.** student's answers. **3.** student's answers. **4.** sleek, sinuous, full-bodied, chasing, chuckling, gripping, gurgle, leaving, laugh, to fling itself, caught, held, a-shake, a-shiver, glints, gleams, sparkles, rustle, swirl, chatter, bubble. **5.** student's answers.

UNIT 25

1. which they, They, it, their, They, their, Their, its, their, you, you. It. **2.** a. It, them. b. It, their. c. their. **3.** student's answers. **4.** student's answers.

UNIT 26

1. First, Second, Next, Now, Meanwhile, Finally. **2.** student's answers. **3.** Beginning: At first, To start with, At the commencement. Middle: After a while, Then, The next thing to do. End: Finally, To conclude, In the end. **4.** student's answers. **5.** student's answers.

UNIT 27

1. The modern orchestra consists of a group of musicians who play various kinds of instruments. In the orchestra the instruments are grouped. Then there is the woodwind family. Next, there are the brass instruments. Finally, there are the percussion instruments. The orchestra, as we know it today, developed in the 17th century. **2.** Then, Next, Finally. **3.** precision./ through it./ demanding./ a ballet./ **4.** student's answers.

UNIT 28

1. Correct words: having, great, here, got to, my, telling, you, He and I, saw, an, night, did, fishing, anything, me, whole, You're. **2.** a. did. b. done. c. did. d. done. e. did. **3.** a. I. b. me. c. me. d. I. e. me. **4.** a. saw. b. seen. c. saw. d. seen. **5.** a. sank. b. sank. c. rang. d. rung. e. sang. **6.** Across: 1. saw. 2. me. 3. seen. 4. rang. 5. done. Down: 1. seen. 2. me. 3. sang. 4. rung. 5. did.

UNIT 29

1. correct words: their, anything, affects, too, anything, assure, from, loan, really, accept, my. **2.** correct words: a. lose, began. b. came, immigrated. c. fewer, dairy. d. lay, laid. e. lend, loan. f. among, is. g. have, rung. **3.** student's answers. **4.** a. saw is correct, it is the past tense of the verb *to see* and *seen* is the past participle and needs the auxiliary verb *to have*. b. sank is correct, it is the past tense of the verb *to sink* and *sunk* is the past participle and needs the auxiliary verb *to have*. c. My is correct, it is a pronominal adjective and shows ownership, me is a personal pronoun.

UNIT 30

1. a. cars. b. stand snorting, pawing the hard earth, they strain to leap at the matador, c. they generally charge at anything red. d. bulls are compared with cars. **2.** a. student's answers. b. student's answers. c. examples: Something to think about. Being boastful. Getting into trouble. Being thorough. Staying up late at night, getting up early in the morning. Telling a secret. Being rash. Impossible task. Not being the important one. Being over particular. **3.** student's answers.

UNIT 31

1. a. Jimbo's, children's sister's, sister's, sisters', sisters', sisters'. b. Dad's, I'm, dad's, He's, dad's, You'll, dad's, dad's, You'd, dad's. **2.** a. dads' arms. b. children's dads. c. Emma's dad, Charlie's. d. sisters' dogs. e. men's arms. **3.** a. don't, they've, That's. b. What's, you're. c. C'mon don't, it's. d. He's, she's. e. Where's, It's. **4.** a. I'm sure that Jimbo's and the other children's stories made them laugh, don't you? b. I've heard tall stories about sports persons' records, haven't you? c. The men's tall stories and the women's tall stories didn't ring true, but we're still laughing, aren't you? **5.** a. women's. b. actors'. c. ladies'. d. Charlie's. e. girls' or girl's depending on whether there are many girls or only one, as in the latter. f. It's. g. no apostrophe needed. h. don't, I'll. i. We've. j. I've.

UNIT 32

1. a. "What's the joke?" b. "Look what Jason did!" "I swear it doesn't!" **2.** The go-cart kids, who lived in the suburbs, were enthusiastic, imaginative, young and active children. Consequently, they had lots of fun adventures and excitement. b. drive: to separate long parts of a sentence and show a pause. Well: to show a pause. else: to separate what was said from the rest of the sentence. **3.** a. "Do you have a go-cart?" asked Tony. "Not me!" exclaimed Andy. "I have a really fast, manoeuverable, red billy-cart, though." b. "Jo's go-cart has stalled on the corner," said Ted. "Oh no!" exclaimed Jason. "What will she do?" **4.** a. Tony asked Andy if he had a go-cart. Andy said that he didn't but he has a really fast manoeuverable red billy-cart. b. Ted said that Jo's go-cart had stalled on the corner. Jason called out and asked Jo what she would do. **5.** a. I race every week; it's fun. b. Bring along these items: a warm sweater, a helmet, goggles, glasses and an old pair of jeans. c. Jed has a new go-cart; it's magnificent! d. The go-cart has a motor, many other items, like a brake, excellent steering mechanism and beautiful ball-bearing wheels. e. I like go-carts; Kim likes billy-carts.

TAKE A TEST 4. REVISION: UNITS 24 – 32

1. a. similar. b. opposite. c. synonyms. d. antonyms. **2.** suggestions: a. lovely, attractive, pretty, elegant. b. quick, rapid, speedy. c. leap, spring, bound, vault. d. intelligent, smart, bright. **3.** a. bad. b. cloudy. c. fat. d. low. **4.** student's answers. **5.** student's answers. **6.** a. signal, next. b. suggestions: then, next, after, later. at last, finally. **7.** a. He and I. b. sang. c. did. d. She and I, saw. e. me. **8.** correct words: a. came, loan. b. among. c. have, rung. **9.** a. dad's. b. children's. c. sisters'. **10.** a. I said "I will see you at the beach." b. "I am going home," I said to her.